World Economics Association

Book Series

Volume 9

D1457304

Narrative Fixation in Economics

Titles produced by the World Economics Association & College Publications

Volume 1:
The Economics Curriculum. Towards a Radical Reformation. Maria Alejandra Madi and Jack Reardon, eds.
Volume 2:
Finance as Warfare. Michael Hudson
Volume 3:
Developing an Economics for the Post-crisis World. Steve Keen
Volume 4:
On the Use and Misuse of Theories and Models in Mainstream Economics. Lars Pålsson Syll
Volume 5:
Green Capitalism. The God that Failed. Richard Smith
Volume 6:
40 Critical Pointers for Students of Economics. Stuart Birks
Volume 7:
The European Crisis. Victor Beker and Beniamino Moro, eds.
Volume 8:
A Philosophical Framework for Rethinking Theoretical Economics and Philosophy of Economics. Gustavo Marqués
Volume 9:
Narrative Fixation in Economics. Edward Fullbrook

The **World Economics Association (WEA)** was launched on May 16, 2011. Already over 13,000 economists and related scholars have joined. This phenomenal success has come about because the WEA fills a huge gap in the international community of economists – the absence of a professional organization which is truly international and pluralist.

The World Economics Association seeks to increase the relevance, breadth and depth of economic thought. Its key qualities are worldwide membership and governance, and inclusiveness with respect to: (a) the variety of theoretical perspectives; (b) the range of human activities and issues which fall within the broad domain of economics; and (c) the study of the world's diverse economies.

The Association's activities centre on the development, promotion and diffusion of economic research and knowledge and on illuminating their social character.

The WEA publishes 20+ books a year, three open-access journals *(Economic Thought, World Economic Review* and *Real-World Economics Review*), a bi-monthly newsletter, blogs, holds global online conferences, runs a textbook commentaries project and an eBook library.

www.worldeconomicassociation.org

Narrative Fixation in Economics

Edward Fullbrook

© Edward Fullbrook, WEA and College Publications 2016.

All rights reserved.

ISBN 978-1-84890-228-2 print
ISBN 978-1-911156-34-5 eBook-PDF

Published by College Publications (London) on behalf of the World Economics Association (Bristol)

http://www.worldeconomicsassociation.org
http://www.collegepublications.co.uk

Cover photo by Kyla Rushman
Cover design by Laraine Welch
Printed by Lightning Source, Milton Keynes, UK

All rights reserved. No part of this publication may be reproduced, stored in a retrieval system or transmitted in any form, or by any means, electronic, mechanical, photocopying, recording or otherwise without prior permission, in writing, from the publisher.

Contents

Preface

Determinism, the idea that everything that happens must happen as it does and could not have happened any other way, and atomism, the idea that the world is made up of entities whose qualities are independent of their relations with other entities, are fundament components of classical mechanics. Atomism is also central to the concept of mind developed in John Locke's *An Essay Concerning Human Understanding*, published (1690) three years after Newton's *Principia*. Locke's general conception of the human mind became commonplace among 18th-century philosophers, so when Adam Smith came to write the foundational text for economics, *The Wealth of Nations* (1776), he had the example not only of Newton's material atomism, but also of Locke's extension of it to an altogether different area of inquiry. If atomism could form the basis of a theory of ideas, then why not apply it as well to a theory of human beings?

Of course Smith did not limit his vision of economic reality to what could be seen through the metaphysical lens of classical mechanics. But a century later the founders of Neoclassical economics did exactly that and even boasted that they were doing so. Their justification of course – and it was a plausible one at the time – was the enormous success that exclusive devotion to this approach had yielded in physics. In time, especially from the 1960s onwards, undivided allegiance to this determinist-atomistic narrative became, with few exceptions, a basic requirement for making a career in economics.

History, however, has shown that there was a great irony in economics' decision to become zealously fixated on taking this particular approach toward economic reality. In the same decades that Neoclassical economics was being created, physics was moving rapidly away from its insistence upon the determinist-atomistic narrative and towards narrative pluralism.

The achievements resulting from this opening up of physics to other narratives have been even more spectacular than those that came from classical mechanics. Without that intellectual liberation, human reality would be radically different from what it is as I write.

But economics – except among a now widening fringe heavily supported by the young – remains locked in the same narrative dogmatism from which physics escaped a century and a half ago. Meanwhile economic evolution has continued. And as the gap between economic reality and the Neoclassical portrayal of it grows ever wider, Neoclassical voices become shriller and their arguments, when placed within the context of the real-world, ever more farcical. Understandably in self-defence, but shamelessly and ultimately at great cost to humanity, economics in its traditional centres moves ever further away from the ethos of science and becomes ever more ruthlessly devoted to scientism.

This book, against the background of modern physics' narrative pluralism, considers the foundations of the single narrative path along which mainstream economics has for so long travelled and the increasingly bizarre narrative to which it has led. As Einstein said, "It is theory which decides what can be observed," and as history's decades pass, what Neoclassical theory enables us to observe becomes less and less, until even colossal economic events on the eve of their happening go unnoticed. Whereas the Global Financial Collapse of 2007 was foreseen years in advance by Baker, Borio, Godley, Hudson, Keen, Pettifor, Richebächer, Roubini, Shiller, Soros, White and other economists not circumscribed by Neoclassicalism, its approach right up to the day of its happening was unobserved by those who were. Meanwhile the economy's death threat to the ecosystem remains for the Neoclassical mainstream an irrelevancy, as do the enormous upward redistributions of income and wealth undermining society's fundamental structures and now giving rise to Trumpism and the new fascism in general. Scientism is always a farce, but in this case it is one leading humanity towards devastation. We, economists and non-economists, urgently need to understand this intellectual cult threatening us all.

Edward Fullbrook,
November 2016

Chapter 1

The narrative pluralism of physics

> "Whether you can observe a thing or not depends on the theory which you use. It is theory which decides what can be observed" (Albert Einstein speaking to Werner Heisenberg during his 1926 Berlin lecture, quoted in Salam 1990).

A. Introduction

Einstein's revolution led philosophers and historians of science to abandon 19th-century views of scientific progress as a smooth accumulation of tested facts. Scholars came to focus instead on the processes by which one theory displaces or subsumes another. By the 1960s, obsession with competing theories became so extreme that increasingly all science was defined and interpreted relative to its infrequent revolutions (Kuhn 1962). This narrative Gestalt has spread through contemporary culture, dominating its perceptions of the advancement of knowledge.

Generally – and the present case is no exception – the natural sciences ignore outsider analysis, but the narrative fixation on the dialectical side of scientific development has had and continues to have a deleterious effect on the human sciences. Of course theory displacement offers a true characterisation of important chapters in science history. But there are many major advances in science for which the narrative of scientific revolutions, including its intervals of "normal science", has no explanatory power. More to the point, in the human sciences those "extraordinary episodes" which have "necessitated the community's rejection of one time-honoured scientific theory in favour of another incompatible with it," are virtually unknown (Kuhn 1962, p. 6). In economics, for example, the absence of such episodes weighs so heavily on its pursuit of understanding that no sensible overview of its fundamental ideas is possible without abandoning the traditional narrative structure.

The notion of *narrative* provides this book and especially this chapter with its central organizing concept. The term is deployed inclusively, so as to encompass everything from the theories of micro physics to the myths of traditional societies. Narratives commonly taught in universities, "knowledge narratives", will receive primary attention. It frequently happens that in a field of empirical enquiry there emerge several narratives which rather than being contradictory or incompatible are complementary in the sense of offering different windows for observation of the same or overlapping domains of phenomena. Every narrative – and, therefore, every theory, paradigm and research program – launches itself from a conceptual framework, including a set of presuppositions about the nature of reality. Inevitably, different conceptual frameworks offer different points of view on the object of inquiry. What one sees when one looks at Michelangelo's statue of *David* depends on the standpoint from which it is observed; similarly, what any empirical inquiry makes of its object depends on the conceptual framework through which it is viewed. Just as full appreciation of *David* requires viewing it from more than one perspective, so knowledge accumulation often depends upon investigating empirical domains through more than one narrative. I call this the doctrine of **narrative pluralism**. It is the same view of empirical understanding that the physicist David Bohm describes as follows.

> "What is called for is not an *integration* of thought, or a kind of imposed unity, for any such imposed point of view would itself be merely another fragment. Rather, all our different ways of thinking are to be considered as different ways of looking at the one reality, each with some domain in which it is clear and adequate. One may indeed compare a theory to a particular view of some object. Each view gives an appearance of the object in some aspect. The whole object is not perceived in any one view but, rather, it is grasped only *implicitly* as that single reality which is shown in all these views. When we deeply understand that our theories also work in this way, then we will not fall into the habit of seeing reality and acting toward it as if it were constituted of

> separately existent fragments corresponding to how it appears in our thought and in our imagination when we take our theories to be 'direct descriptions of reality as it is'" (Bohm 1983, pp. 7-8).

The details of these and related arguments will be set out in three sections. First, the narrative function of conceptual frameworks will be explained by examining their various standard elements. Second, modern physics will be surveyed as an exemplary case of narrative pluralism and its benefits. Third, narrative pathologies common to the social sciences and a consequence of anti-pluralism or narrative fixation will be identified.

B. Narrative selection

1. Simplification

"[E]xperience has to organize," wrote Henry James, "some system of observation – for fear, in the immensity, of losing its way" (James 1962, p. 3). At the social level, this path finding embodies itself in various forms of representation: maps, verbal accounts, formulae, systems of equations, graphs, pictures, etc. All representations, whatever their form, proceed on the basis of a simplification of reality. There are no exceptions to this rule, not even the most sophisticated scientific theories. Jorge Luis Borges's parable "Of Exactitude in Science" illustrates the folly of disregarding this most fundamental of all narrative principles.

> "... In that Empire, the craft of Cartography attained such Perfection that the Map of a Single province covered the space of an entire City, and the Map of the Empire itself an entire Province. In the course of Time, these Extensive maps were found somehow wanting, and so the College of Cartographers evolved a Map of the Empire that was of the same Scale as the Empire and coincided with it point for point. Less attentive to the Study of Cartography, succeeding Generations came to judge a map of such Magnitude cumbersome, and, not without Irreverence, they

> abandoned it to the Rigours of sun and Rain. In the western Deserts, tattered Fragments of the Map are still to be found, Sheltering an occasional Beast or beggar; in the whole Nation, no other relic is left of the Discipline of Geography" (Borges 1975, p. 131).

But charming and useful as it is, Borges's parable illustrates only one aspect of any representation's need for simplification. For every empirical domain there exists an infinity of possible points of view and, therefore, also of potential observations. These plethoras of possibilities, together with the dilemma posed by Borges, present observers/narrators with an acute problem of choice. They must decide which features of their domains they are going to describe and which they are going to disregard. Each of their narratives can proceed only on the basis of a radical simplification of reality. To this end, and in lieu of random observations from random points of view, narrators deploy principles of selection, or what James called "systems of observation" and today's writers usually call "conceptual frameworks". This process abstracts certain features of the narrative's domain while ignoring others. A narrative may make explicit its narrative framework, but more often it leaves it partly or wholly concealed, leaving it to operate outside critical awareness.

We must not forget that knowledge narratives, no less than popular and literary ones, explore reality by simplifying it. They obscure great masses of detail, so as to systematically highlight certain aspects of that reality which a group of individuals have identified as being of special interest to themselves. Different but non-competing narratives of the same domain give prominence to different dimensions of that domain. Each narrative functions as an interpretative system, as a *special* way of perceiving some corner of existence.

Narrative selection proceeds through a set of assumptions which simplify or pre-empt many features of the narrative's domain. These assumptions include a system of classification of entities, the attribution of a limited number of properties to those entities, some metaphysic which posits a kind or kinds of connection between events, and usually the recognition of different structural levels within the domain of inquiry. A narrative also views its domain from a certain scale, omitting details that it sees as too microscopical or too global, too short-run or too long-run. Typically it also describes its domain within some range of accuracy or approximation, ignoring effects which do not fall within that range. Finally, every knowledge narrative has its community of practitioners, people who develop and deploy the narrative in writing and teaching. As socially, economically, geo-politically and historically situated individuals, these people bring to the narrative enterprise various inclinations and sensibilities, as well as overt purposes, all of which help determine which aspects of the domain the narrative includes, emphasizes and ignores.

2. Classification

Wittgenstein noted that "*The limits of my language* mean the limits of my world," and that "what we cannot think we cannot *say* either" (Wittgenstein 1974, 5.6, 5.61). Our categories of thought, including our groupings of the objects of the world, pervade our descriptive use of language and organize all our experience. Even the predicates of everyday language categorize, though not always very precisely, the contents of the world. These informal classifications, with their mixtures of the personal and the cultural, are the means by which we order the perceptual fields of our daily existences. Similarly, every narrative needs to provide some classification of the objects in its domain.

In the specialized narratives of science this shaping of the facts is especially pronounced because the number of categories tends to be strictly limited. The selection of categories inevitably involves arbitrariness because there exists countless numbers of objectively grounded ways in which the contents of a domain can be categorized. Another parable from Borges illustrates this inescapable aspect of narratives. An Argentinean consults an imaginary Chinese encyclopaedia which says that "animals are divided into: (a) belonging to the Emperor, (b) embalmed, (c) tame, (d) sucking pigs), (e) sirens, (f) fabulous, (g) stray dogs, (h) included in the present classification, (i) frenzied, (j) innumerable, (k) drawn with a very fine camel-hair brush, (l) et cetera, (m) having just broken the water pitcher, (n) that from a long way off look like flies" (Foucault, 1971, p. 2).

The outlandishness of Borges's imaginary taxonomy of the animal kingdom, as well as the ambiguity of its selection criteria, suggests the diversity of ways in which one can, without forgoing objective grounding, categorize a sector of reality. Make-believe classifications, however, are not alone in making manifest the arbitrariness of conceptual orders and their resulting perceptual fields. Ethnological studies offer numerous examples of zoological classifications whose non-essential nature is immediately obvious to outsiders. Consider the case of the villagers of Baan Phraan Muan in north-eastern Thailand. They divide the animal kingdom on the basis of two criteria: edibility and habitat (Tamiah 1969). These generate five major primary categories: insects (inedible), birds (edible), water animals (edible), animals of the house and village (animals in the house are inedible, animals under the house are edible) and forest animals (animals of the deep forest are inedible and other forest animals are edible unless they have domesticated counterparts in the house). But these criteria leave numerous organisms known to the Muan standing awkwardly alone in their own primary classes and rivalling Borges's for their apparent fancifulness. These anomalies include house rat (only small children eat), field rat (only small children eat; adults eat privately), giant lizard (medicinal food for children), monitor lizard (edible, but dangerous to mothers after childbirth), chameleon (medicinal food), snake (inedible), vulture (inedible) and crow (inedible).

The Karam people of New Guinea also use habitat as one of the two criteria by which they classify the animal world (Bulmer 1967). But their notion of habitat differs from that of the villagers of Muan in being two-dimensional. Its horizontal axis has the forest at one pole, the homestead at the other and open country and gardens in between. Its vertical axis runs from aerial through arboreal, terrestrial and aquatic, to subterranean. The Karam's second set of criteria are morphological (physiological): winged or wingless; bony or boneless; bipedal, quadrupedal, multipedal or limbless; elongated or not; and large, medium-sized or small. These two sets of criteria divide the Karam's zoological world into 94 primary categories. One of these, flying birds and bats, contains 44 percent of the Karam's 422 named organisms, whereas another includes only tadpoles.

Cultural bias may incline us to attribute the disparateness between the Muan's and the Karam's ways of dividing up the animal world as due to their common absence of a scientific basis. More especially, we might expect that modern biology with its grounding in evolutionary theory, would provide for animals a determinate and definitive classification. But that is not the case. Science teaches us that the evolutionary process abounds with ambiguities. It is not even clear what are the units that survive or become extinct. Are they genes, fragments of genes, chromosomes, genotypes, phenotypes, groups of organisms, gene pools or species? This assortment of possible basic units has generated various formulations, offering different points of view on the selection process. It is this family of narratives which comprises modern evolutionary biology.

Nor does nature's biological ambiguity as revealed by science end here. Not one but numerous concepts of "species" have emerged from evolutionary theory (Dupré 1993, pp. 37-59). These concepts divide into two types, the "biological" and the "phylogenetic". The former defines a species as "a group of organisms connected to one another by actual or possible reproductive links, and reproductively isolated from other organisms" (Dupré, p. 46). Though we may find the biological species concept intuitively satisfying, it is inapplicable to asexual organisms and, therefore, to most micro-organisms and, therefore, to microbiology. Phylogenetic taxonomies, on the other hand, have as their basic principle that the organisms forming a species should descend from a common set of "ancestors". But in an evolutionary context this condition obviously is not sufficient. Rules are needed to identify cut-off points in the lines of descent, and to establish "what makes a genealogically coherent set of organisms correspond to the rank of species" (Dupré, p. 48). To this end, various criteria, each leading to a different classification, have been put forward and used in modern biology.

The plurality of possible basic units of selection and the diverse concepts of "species", however, are neither the only nor the most profound manifestation of pluralism in the classification of organisms in biology today. In ecological biology, niche, not species, is the basic classificatory unit. The idea of niche more resembles the Muan's and the Karam's implicit concept of habitat than it does any of evolutionary biology's notions of species. Frequently more than one species can perform the role required of a particular ecological niche. Consequently, ecological-based classifications of organisms differ greatly from evolutionary-based ones (Dupré, pp. 43, 58).

Finally, a brief example from Thomas Kuhn will reinforce much that has just been said. It reveals two different classificatory concepts for "molecule" concurrently and productively at work in the physical sciences. Kuhn relates the responses of a "distinguished physicist and an eminent chemist" when asked whether a single atom of helium was or was not a molecule.

> "Both answered without hesitation, but their answers were not the same. For the chemist the atom of helium was a molecule because it behaved like one with respect to the kinetic theory of gases. For the physicist, on the other hand, the helium atom was not a molecule because it displayed no molecular spectrum. Presumably both men were talking of the same particle, but they were viewing it through their own research training and practice. Undoubtedly their experiences had had much in common, but they did not, in this case, tell the two specialists the same thing" (Kuhn 1970, pp. 50-1).

The gist of this and of our other examples of classification can now be summarized. Borges's zoological fantasy, by means of what are from conventional viewpoints its glaring omissions, called our attention to how any classification of an empirical domain limits the possible descriptions, and thereby also the field of possible facts and possible questions. Similarly, without discounting their epistemological value for the cultural-geographical situations to which they are applied, the alien taxonomies the Muan and the Karam encourage us to recognize the indeterminateness and contingency of all classifications of empirical realms. But we also have seen from examples from contemporary biology that even when it comes to dividing up a domain on the basis of the most advanced science there exist more than one plausible and defensible way of doing so. *The best way will depend on the purposes of the narrative for which the classification is intended.* Every categorization of a set of empirical phenomena uniquely circumscribes our possible understanding of that realm of reality, rather as every position which one takes up around Michelangelo's statue of David limits what one can see. Likewise the numerous ways in which any domain can be divided up, means that there exist many different bases for making a systematic inquiry of that domain.

3. Selection of properties

Of all narrative genres, ontologies are the most elemental because they make assertions about the fundamental nature of reality--about what sorts of entities, properties and relations compose existence. But all narratives, and especially knowledge narratives, postulate a sort of proto-ontology in the sense of identifying a certain range of phenomena (a "universe of discourse") whose existence, real or imagined, they wish to take into account. In the formation of these proto-ontologies, the classification of entities typically requires the predication of various properties, making these two processes inextricably intertwined. This conceptual interdependency is especially pronounced in the more narrowly focused physical sciences, which, from out of the welter of phenomenological possibilities emanating from some empirical domain, abstract a very limited set of phenomena for cognitive attention.

Highly specialized proto-ontologies are commonplace in the study of physical matter. Consider the case of crystallography, the scientific study of crystals. It divides solid bodies into two classes: crystals and non-crystals. This division presumes certain properties – approximately plane geometrical surfaces with straight edges which meet other such planes, thus bounding the object on all sides – which identify some materials as belonging to the crystal category. Along with six kinds of symmetry (mirroring, inversion, and twofold, threefold, fourfold and sixfold rotations) these properties – not mass and extension or chemical composition or market-value – are the fundamental properties of the crystallography narrative. These selected attributes divide the class of all crystals into 32 subclasses. The result is a powerful but quite limited descriptive system, one of many useful frameworks of classes and properties for viewing solid objects.

A classification of objects leads to further questions about what additional characteristics of the entities classified should the narrative recognize. For example, in regarding material substance, classical mechanics includes the properties of mass and length, but not the symmetrical properties of crystals or the colligative properties of solutions. The immensity and richness of actuality compels even the most comprehensive narratives to exclude more characteristics than they include. For this reason, the descriptions of any narrative are always stylized abstractions of reality. Nor is it only knowledge narratives which are characterized by this sort of abstraction. All narratives, even Joyce's *Ulysses* and Proust's *Remembrances of Things Past*, take shape on the basis of radical exclusion of phenomenal detail. The Nigerian philosopher and anthropologist Robin Horton illustrates this narrative principle at work both in traditional African religion and in modern science.

> "Thus when traditional thought draws upon people and their social relations as the raw material of its theoretical models, it makes use of some dimensions of human life and neglects others. The definition of a god may omit any reference to his physical appearance, his diet, his mode of lodging, his children, his relations with his wives, and so on. Asking questions about such attributes is as inappropriate as asking questions about the colour of a molecule or the temperature of an electron. It is this omission of many dimensions of human life from the definition of the gods which give them that rarefied, attenuated aura which we call 'spirituality'. It is the result of the same process of abstraction as the one we see at work in Western theoretical models: the process whereby features of the prototype phenomena which have explanatory relevance are incorporated into a theoretical schema, while features which lack such relevance are omitted" (Horton 1971, p. 225).

This idea of "explanatory relevance" suggests a further dimension of conceptual frameworks, namely the inclusion of some basis for conceiving connections between various categories of phenomena and their properties.

4. Interconnectivity: ten kinds of narrative linkage

Narratives need notions about how the things they classify and describe are connected. "[T]he most usual species of connection," said David Hume, "among the different events which enter into any narrative composition is that of cause and effect" (Hume 1955, p. 34). The relation of causation holds between two events when, given the occurrence of one event, it results in a second. The putative causal event may be either natural or supernatural, and the relation may be postulated either as a general rule as in the laws of chemistry and the procedures of witchcraft or as a singularity as with events in a novel. Causal linkages make phenomena fall into configurations, enabling us to apprehend various items as contributing to an interrelated system of parts or forming an intelligible pattern of events. This showing of things leading to other things distinguishes narratives from mere listings, descriptions and chronological sequences. I wish to consider these cause and effect linkages with regard to five criteria:

1. whether they explain in terms of past or future events,
2. whether these explanations are open or closed in the sense of admitting or not admitting indeterminacies,
3. whether they explain a property of something as due only to that something's parts or due also to the structure by which those parts are organized,
4. whether they explain the whole in terms of its parts or vice-versa,
5. whether between entities they postulate internal or external relations.

a. Teleological and non-teleological explanations

Time's linearity leads to two basic methods of framing narrative connections between events happening at separate moments. Items may be explained in terms of their consequences, as when we say Othello fell on his sword because he wanted to die. Alternately, an explanation may run in the other direction, the consequences explained in terms of some prior event, as when we say Othello died because he fell on his sword. Explanations of the former type are called teleological or functional and find frequent use with respect to human actions. Such usage arises from regarding humans as purposive beings, a view which obliges us to explain their behaviour, at least in part, as a function of wishes to bring about various future events. Consequently, the human sciences abound with narratives which explain operations in terms of their consequences. But the range of knowledge narratives which rely heavily on functional linkage is much broader than this, and it is examples from outside the human sciences that I want to emphasize here.

Functional or teleological narratives interpret processes from the perspective of "wholes" or systems of interconnected components desiring or designed for the achievement of some end, in other words, a future event. Such narratives focus attention on culminations and consequences, and link the behaviour of each component to the end or purpose of the whole or system to which it belongs. Physiology is a well-known example of a primarily teleological knowledge narrative. It proceeds by identifying the function an organ performs for its organism and how it works to that end. Likewise, more often than not we perceive human artefacts, especially advanced technology, through functional or teleological narratives. A comb is a device for untangling hair; an automobile is a mechanism for getting about in and, sometimes, for impressing one's neighbours. Functional analysis identifies and classifies an entity's parts in terms of their sub-functions. For example, we commonly analyze an automobile into its various parts – a fuel system, an ignition system, a carburettor, some combustion chambers with pistons, a crankshaft, a transmission, a chassis, a set of wheels, a steering wheel, a breaking system, and seats – and explain them in terms of their contribution to the intended function of the whole. The same kind of teleological account pertains to a system's subcomponents and their operations. Continuing with the car example, a science dictionary tells us that the crankshaft is an "essential component of piston engines that converts the up-and-down (reciprocating) motion of the pistons into useful rotary motion" (Lafferty and Rose 1994, p. 159). The entry then explains how the components of the crankshaft work to this end. Technological culture could not exist without narratives of this type.

Proceeding from the other direction, non-teleological explanations focus attention on the conditions and events preceding the event, process or state of affairs being explained.

> "They seek to exhibit the integrated behaviours of complex systems as the resultants of more elementary factors, frequently identified as constituent parts of those systems; and they are therefore concerned with traits of complex wholes almost exclusively to the extent that these traits are dependent on assumed characteristics of the elementary factors" (Hempel 1966, p. 93).

For example, under this narrative mode the crankshaft's conversion of reciprocating motion into rotary motion is interpreted in terms of the laws of mechanics, the firing of the pistons, and the initial conditions constituted by the crank pins, the connecting rods and bearings, and the crankshaft.

b. Closed and open narratives

Turn now to another, more difficult, and more provocative aspect of narrative linkage, the distinction between determinate and indeterminate explanations. Some narratives are *closed* in the sense that they describe all their events as predetermined, whereas others are *open* in the sense that they admit indeterminacies. Narratives divide between these two categories. Those of the closed or determinate variety claim that give X, Y must follow, whereas open or indeterminate narratives explain Y in terms of X without the presumption that Y *always* follows X. If a field of inquiry is not seen as wholly determinate, meaning that chance, contingency, choice, uncertainty, randomness, or spontaneity enter into the relations between events, then the sets of events open to explanation by the determinate and indeterminate approaches are not coextensive. With these different ranges of application, the choice between the two forms of narrative linkage is one of selecting a method appropriate to the perceived subject matter. As such, this question of finding a suitable narrative form must not be conflated with the metaphysical question of whether reality in general is determinate or not. Traditionally philosophers have lavished attention on the latter question, but for us it need not be at issue. Here we want merely to consider two types of narrative linkage, two conceptual angles offering different vantage points on the field of observation. As I will illustrate, within the same domain of inquiry both types of explanation may prove useful. Like the hammer and saw, the use of one conceptual tool does not preclude the use of the other.

To place these joint notions of open and closed narratives in a more traditionalist context, consider Popper's definition of a physically closed system.

> "By a physically closed system I mean a set or system of physical entities ... which interact with each other – and *only* with each other – in accordance with definite laws of

> interaction that do not leave any room for interaction with, or interference by, anything outside that closed set or system of physical entities" (Popper 1972, p. 219).

This definition, when modified as follows, defines a closed or determinate narrative. By a closed narrative I mean an account of a set or system of entities and their interactions with each other – and *only* with each other – in terms of definite laws of interaction that do not leave any room for interaction with, or interference by, anything outside that closed set or system of entities.

Tolerance for open or indeterminate narratives, however, is very much a modern development. Robin Horton notes that in the traditional cultures of Africa, the concept of coincidence or chance scarcely exists.

> "When a rotten branch falls off a tree and kills a man walking underneath it, there has to be a definite explanation of the calamity. Perhaps the man quarrelled with a half brother over some matter of inheritance, and the latter worked the fall of the branch through a sorcerer. Or perhaps he misappropriated lineage property, and the lineage ancestors brought the branch down on his head. *The idea that the whole thing could have come about through the accidental convergence of two independent chains of events is inconceivable because it is psychologically intolerable.* To entertain it would be to admit that the episode was inexplicable and unpredictable: a glaring confession of ignorance" (italics added) (Horton 1971, p. 250).

But Western culture also has exercised a strong bias against open narratives. This partiality, which until a century and a half ago was hegemonic, owes more than a little to Aristotle. His *Poetics* scorned narratives whose episodes "follow each other without any probable or necessary connection," and applauded the *Odyssey* and the *Iliad* for the manner in which their events are "connected into one event" (Aristotle 1934, Part II, sec. V). With incomparable influence, Aristotle argued that actions "should arise from the structure of the fable itself, so as to be the natural consequences, necessary or probable, of what has preceded in the action" (Aristotle 1934, Part II, sec. VIII). Moreover, "the fable ... should be an imitation of an action that is one and entire, the parts of it being so connected that if any one of them be either transposed or taken away, the whole will be destroyed or changed" (Aristotle 1934, Part II, sec. V). Determinism as embodied in many scientific theories is but a variation of this ancient sensibility regarding narrative and the connection of events. Newtonian mechanics, especially as reworked by Laplace, achieves perfect "unity of action". Given the positions and velocities of all the particles at any one moment, this narrative's system of equations determines the positions and velocities, and thereby the actions, of all particles for all moments, both future and past. With every event portrayed as part of an unbroken chain of events, if any one of them fails to take place, then the whole scientific narrative would, in effect, "be destroyed".

Horton's example of the falling tree branch, however, suggests that some happenings may not, at least from an epistemological point of view, always best be described and understood as emanating from a single and predetermined chain of events. Observation may repeatedly reveal gaps in such chains or chance convergences of two or more such chains, showing elements of unpredictability or randomness in reality. Historically these indeterminacies have proven no less "psychologically intolerable" to many scientists and philosophers of science than they have to members of traditional African cultures. The willingness of the cultural elites of Western societies to engage with open narratives is an even more recent development than their willingness to engage with democratic processes. Prior to Darwin, no space existed in scientific narratives for indeterminate phenomena. This dimension of reality was barred from scientific inquiry no less than was heliocentric cosmology under the popes. "The doctrine of scientific determinism," writes Stephen Hawking, "remained the standard assumption of science until the early years of this century" (Hawking 1995, p. 59). As a physicist, Hawking thinks of quantum mechanics as the breakthrough narrative, but biologists have the better claim to being the first natural scientists to develop an open narrative that successfully breached the determinist hegemony. Evolutionary theory from Wallace (1858) and Darwin (1859) onwards relies heavily on indeterminacy as a narrative linkage.

Neo-Darwinism, which combines natural selection with Mendelian genetics and whose advent was roughly contemporaneous with the development of quantum mechanics, exemplifies open knowledge narratives. Neo-Darwinism admits indeterminacy at several levels. It predicates two sources of heritable variation, both conceptually conceived as indeterminate processes. First, the genes of each individual are the result of a random shuffle of existing genetic material (genetic recombination). Second, random mutational jumps occur due to accidents in replication and repair of DNA, accidents now attributed largely to cosmic rays modifying gene structures. Natural selection operates on these randomly shuffled and mutating genes within the field of a changing environment. The evolutionary narrative also treats this form of variation as indeterminate, as resulting from both random non-biological causes – for example, meteorites, volcanic eruptions, continental drift – and from the indeterminate and recursive process of natural selection itself. Modern evolutionary biology includes these indeterminate narrative linkages as well as determinate ones from the laws of inheritance, most especially that *in every case* mixtures of characteristics inherited from the parents do not blend but remain distinct.

Despite the development in the natural sciences of hugely successful narratives embracing "concepts which formally recognize the existence of various kinds of limitation upon the possible completeness of explanation and prediction" (Horton 1971, p. 250) there remain scientists and philosophers who retain a nostalgia for Newtonian certainties. The vision of a clockwork universe – no less than one governed by ubiquitous spiritual agency – is a dream not easily foregone. For those wedded to the metaphysics of determinism, quantum mechanics is but a halfway house to perfect knowledge, while evolutionary theory scarcely qualifies as science, it being so "riddled" with indeterminacies. But metaphysical belief aside, the open narratives of quantum mechanics and evolutionary biology are the biggest success stories of modern science, especially as applied to the practicalities of technology. For better or worse, we live on the eve of the brave new world of genetic engineering, whereas already quantum mechanics, notes Hawking, "governs the behaviour of transistors and integrated circuits, which are the essential components of electronic devices such as televisions and computers, and is also the basis of modern chemistry and biology" (p. 62).

c. External and internal relations

We need to consider briefly a further aspect of causality which impacts on the distinction between closed and open narratives. This is the question of whether or not a narrative admits internal, as well as external, relations. A narrative may be mechanistic in the sense that the internal structures of its fundamental elements are independent of one another, the elements being connected by only external relationships. The classic detective novel, with its resolution worked out in terms of interactions between unchanging characters, exemplifies this type of narrative linkage. So too does Newton's mechanics, where the causal relations of collision and gravity leave the particles atomistically intact. Internal relations, on the other hand, are "identity-affecting" (Bhaskar 1986, p. 111). Interactions between characters in a literary novel, for example, usually bring about "character development". The description of internally related phenomena has been even more central to the modern development of the natural sciences. This is illustrated by evolutionary theory, which is the story of how the identities of biology's primary units change through interaction.

d. Aggregative versus structural properties

There exist two primary ways of explaining properties. Some narratives explain the properties of things as simply the function of the properties of their parts. For example, engineering treats an object's mass as merely an additive function of the masses of its parts, and the floor space of the Empire State Building as the sum of the floor spaces of its various rooms. Properties explained in this way, I will call *aggregative*. Some knowledge narratives deploy only this approach in their conceptualisation of properties. For example, classical mechanics is based on only three properties – mass, length and time – and with each described in terms of an additive function. Further or "derived" properties are defined in terms of these three primary "dimensions", as for example, velocity is length divided by time, and momentum is mass times length divided by time. Thus, although classical mechanics includes an extensive of list of properties, they all reduce to some mathematical combination of the three primary aggregative properties.

There exist, however, many things possessed of properties which are not properties of their components, but instead come to exist only through the structures by which things are combined. Therefore many fields, and especially the biological sciences, include properties explained as the due to the characteristics of the *structure* by which something's components are combined, rather than as an aggregation of micro-properties. The property of being able to see, for example, is explained not just in terms of the various individual cells of the eye and brain – none of which have the property of being able to see – but also in terms of the way those cells are combined. Similarly, human crowd behaviour is understood as depending on the relations holding between the individuals as well as on the individuals themselves. Although it was Newton's dream that some day all of existence could be accounted for in terms of aggregate properties, modern science has tended to involve itself ever more with structural properties. Even physics, with its various field theories, today concerns itself fundamentally with structural explanation.

e. Direction of causation: micro or macro

Reality presents various levels of complexity, running from atomistic individuals to the universe. This polarity entails two possible directions of narrative explanation: accounting for the more complex in terms of the less so or vice-versa. The first approach, "micro explanation", characterizes Newtonian physics and for several centuries dominated the natural sciences. Chemistry, for example, advanced by describing the decomposition of compound substances by chemical processes into simpler compounds or into their constituent elements. But sometimes the object of inquiry begs a macro approach, as when a property of an individual thing appears mediated or determined by the whole or ensemble of which it is a part. The facts that I grew up speaking English instead of Chinese and eating with a knife and fork instead of chop sticks, for example, seem more attributable to the family and society in which I emerged than to any aspect of my individual make-up. Likewise, when I die, although the event will fit some micro explanation such as heart-failure or perforation of the intestine, the complex changes that will then befall the millions of cells out of which I am composed will be seen to be due to the regrettable change in the whole to which they belong.

Because the metaphysics that grew out of Newtonian science was for so long hegemonic, even today there persist pockets of prejudice against the use of macro linkages in knowledge narratives. Yet science has long conceived of some quantitative properties, such as angle and probability, as based on macro relations. Thus any change in the size of a deck of cards causes every card's probability of being drawn to change. Even more noteworthy is that in physics itself, quantum mechanics has forced through innovations in the use of narrative linkages, placing macro explanation on an equal footing with the older micro variety. The quantum factor, explains the physicist Paul Davies, "denies that the world can be understood in terms of its components alone." Davies continues:

> "the reality of the subatomic particle cannot be untangled from the environment it inhabits... Evidently the macroscopic and the microscopic worlds are intimately interwoven. There is no hope of building a full understanding of matter from the constituent particles alone. Only the system *as a whole* gives concrete expression to microscopic reality. The big and the small co-exist. One does not subsume wholly the other, nor does the other wholly 'explain' the one" (Davies 1995, p. 39).

C. The narrative pluralism of modern physics

In the economics profession there appears to be a common and ingrained misconception regarding the role and nature of pluralism in the natural sciences. If asked whether the statement "Physics has a long tradition of encouraging pluralism" is true or false, many economists would, I suspect, answer "false". So I feel obliged to present some more primary examples directly from the literature of physics to show that this view is fundamentally mistaken. I am concerned with the period roughly from the 1880s to the present. For evidence I will, in addition to Einstein, Bohm and Davies, look at what four other preeminent physicists, who together roughly span this period, have said regarding pluralism in physics.

I begin with Heinrich **Hertz** [1857-1894]. Hertz was first to detect the electromagnetic waves predicted by Maxwell's unification of electricity and magnetism. Subsequently Hertz wrote a textbook, *The Principles of Mechanics Presented in a New Form.* In it he offered a new theoretical framework congenial to the new developments. In the book's introduction, intended for advanced physics students, he sets out what he understands to be the prevailing epistemological ethos in his profession in the late 19th century. He writes:

> "In endeavouring thus to draw inferences as to the future from the past, we always adopt the following process. We form for ourselves images or symbols of external objects... The images of which we here speak are *our conceptions of things*" (Heisenberg 1962, p. 154).
>
> "... various images of the same objects are possible, and these images may differ in various respects..." (Heisenberg 1962, p. 155).
>
> "... we cannot decide without ambiguity whether an image is appropriate or not; ... One image may be more suitable for one purpose, another for another..." (Heisenberg 1962, p. 156).

It is important to understand that Hertz was not making a case for pluralism here, but instead merely describing to the physics student the basis of *the ethos of narrative pluralism* that he saw as characterizing his profession, and thereby as being the context into which his book was introducing a "new system of mechanical principles", a new "mode of conception", a new "mode of treatment", a new "mode of thought". All those are Hertz's phrases.

A second account of the operation of pluralism in physics is provided by Louis **de Broglie** [1892-1987], one of the principal founders of particle physics. He writes as follows:

> "... the quantum of action compels us today to employ 'complementary' descriptions to account for the phenomena

> on the atomic scale. By this term we are to understand descriptions which are certainly complementary but at the same time, taken strictly, incompatible ... ; each of these complementary descriptions is an 'idealiztion' *permitting us to present certain aspects of the phenomena under consideration, but not all the aspects*" (emphasis added).
>
> "The best known instance of such complementary descriptions is supplied by the two descriptions of Matter and Light by means of waves on the one hand and of corpuscles on the other. The employment of each idea... *has proved essential for the interpretation of some phenomenon or other*; but the two ideas still remain, despite every effort, incapable of being reduced to terms of the other, and the only connection that can be established between them is of a statistical nature" (emphasis added) (Broglie, p. 277).

This is an even more robust pluralism than the one Hertz describes, as it identifies the necessity of deploying within the same domain theories that are *incompatible*.

Werner **Heisenberg**'s [1901-1976] understanding of the need for an ongoing pluralism is perhaps even more radical. He writes:

> "... it was found that already in the theory of electricity an analysis using these concepts was no longer possible, and therefore in the investigation of this new domain of experience there emerged new systems of concepts leading to a final mathematical formulation of the laws of electricity."

And then speaking generally of systems of concepts and laws, Heisenberg writes:

> "...we cannot expect [its] concepts and laws to be suitable for the subsequent description of new realms of experience. It is only in this limited sense that quantum-theoretical

> concepts and laws can be considered as final, and only in this limited sense can it ever happen that scientific knowledge is finally formulated in mathematical or, for that matter, in any other language" (Heisenberg 1962, p. 27).

And there is a quote from near the end of Heisenberg's life that is very close to the Einstein quote with which this chapter began.

> "What we observe is not nature itself, but nature exposed to our method of questioning" (Wikiquote).

The leaders of the next generation of physicists continued to emphasize the importance of pluralist practice *as a basic requirement for the advancement of their science*. For example, Richard **Feynman** [1918-1988], celebrated for expanding the theory of quantum electrodynamics and particle theory, spoke to his students as follows in one of his published lectures.

> "As long as physics is incomplete, and we are trying to understand the other laws, then the different possible formulations may give clues about what might happen in other circumstances."

and

> "We must always keep all the alternative ways of looking at a thing in our heads, so physicists ... pay but little attention to the precise reasoning from fixed axioms.
>
> One of the amazing characteristics of nature is the variety of interpretational schemes which is possible" (Feynman 1965, pp. 53-54).

The direct contradiction between the basic concepts of relativity and quantum theory, the pinnacles of physics, has almost inevitably led physicists both to emphasize *pluralism's necessity for advancement of scientific knowledge* and to articulate the epistemological logic underlying the criterion of "appropriateness" asserted by Hertz.

This pluralist tradition in modern physics has, however, been somewhat obscured by the noble efforts of philosophers and historians to epistemologically explain to the non-physicist the Einsteinian revolution. Until the appearance of Einstein's theory of relativity (1905; 1915), Newtonian mechanics with its theory of gravity was unrivalled as the most celebrated theory in the history of science. Its verification by countless experiments and astronomical observations supported the prevailing view of science as a smooth accumulation of facts generated by the application of well-tested theories. So inevitably the discrediting of Newton's theory dismayed and shocked the cultural psyche, traumatizing 20th-century thought about scientific advance and fixating its attention on events structurally resembling the Einsteinian revolution.

Initially there was strong resistance to Einstein's new narratives of gravitation and cosmology, Newton's theory of absolute space and absolute time having for so long been accepted as an unquestionable truth. But following the solar eclipse of 1919, when Einstein's predictions were confirmed by two teams of astronomers, there began a cultural shift regarding the nature of scientific progress. Philosophers and historians of science especially faced a new narrative challenge. The historical situation no longer pressed them to account for continuity in science nor permitted them to characterize science as a process whereby new certainties are endlessly added to existing ones. Instead they struggled to identify and describe the processes by which one theory could or should replace or withstand a challenge from another. The first major work to recast the narrative of scientific progress in terms of *competing theories* was Karl Popper's *The Logic of Scientific Discovery* published in German in 1934.

Popper showed that no amount of verification and inductive support can ever prove a theory. Instead every theory always remains vulnerable to refutation and replacement by another. This was a narrative which nicely accommodated the recent astounding events in physics. Popper's account of theory replacement spelled out various methods, including degrees of falsifiability (Popper 1959, pp. 135, 112-135) empirical content (pp. 119-123), degrees of simplicity (pp. 136-145) and degrees of corroboration (pp. 251-282), for judging between competing theories. Under Popper's narrative of scientific discovery, competing theories fight it out on the basis of these criteria of scientific merit, and the "best" one wins.

From the 1960s onwards Popper's version of the new narrative of scientific progress increasingly came under attack. Thomas Kuhn's *The Structure of Scientific Revolutions* (1962) denied the historical efficacy of Popper's objective criteria for theory-replacement, arguing instead that competing theories or "paradigms" are often incommensurable and that sociological factors, rather than epistemological ones, often determine whether one theory is or is not replaced by another. Imre Lakatos's "Falsification and the Methodology of Scientific Research Programmes" (1970) argued that refuted theories may continue to be used if no better theory exists. Paul Feyerabend's "Against Method" (1970) emphasized that all observation is "theory-laden" and contended that no set of methodological rules can account for theory-replacement and that all knowledge claims are relativistic. But these and other alternatives to Popperian falsification were variations of the basic narrative which had emerged as the natural aftermath of Einstein's revolution. Each added to the collection and interpretation of historical science data to answer questions suggested by the competing-theories narrative. Almost inevitably the decades of debate on theory-replacement has had as its primary effect the deepening and widening of our culture's general perception of scientific progress as the outcome of a struggle between competing theories.

This book, and this chapter in particular, challenges not the narrative of competing theories as such, but rather the hegemony which that narrative maintains over our vision of science. That that narrative fits important chapters in science, including the momentous one which inspired it, is above dispute. But there is much more to conceptual science than just the postulation of frameworks which challenge other frameworks. Formulation of scientific narratives is also about gaining new points of view on domains of inquiry. Viewing the domain from a new conceptual perspective may yield not only additional information but also a new dimension to the understanding of it. The new viewpoint may even reveal fundamental phenomena which were but dimly observable or not observable at all when *looking through a prior conceptual system*. That such new knowledge may be conceptually incommensurable with that acquired through another narrative lens should be regarded not as a scandal but rather as due to *the nature of conceptual thinking*. Except in the special case where two narratives make conflicting predictions, incommensurability between narratives does not argue for competitiveness between them. To the contrary, observing a domain of inquiry through more than one conceptual framework is eminently desirable, as is observing Michelangelo's *David* from more than one standpoint.

Phenomena observed through different conceptual systems may eventually be reconciled through a "deeper" level of theory (like a "bird's-eye view"), as with Maxwell's unification of electronic and magnetic theory. *But such unification can never happen except where narrative pluralism first prevails for that domain of inquiry.*

The narrative of competing theories, especially Kuhn's version, seriously underestimates the scientific imagination, that talent which John Stuart Mill characterized as the faculty for "mentally arranging known elements into new combinations" (Mill 1893, p. 433). Kuhn's narrative assumes that the scientific mind is so deficient in agility as to be incapable of alternating freely between incommensurable conceptual systems. I would be the last to deny that examples of this stereotype exist in every discipline and that in some disciplines this intellectual ineptitude dominates. Nor do I deny that narrative communities sometimes exist in bondage to their conceptual system because they have failed to make explicit its primary presuppositions. But it seems a cruel travesty of the truth to portray the scientist in general as, on the one hand, an intellectual bumpkin, incapable of shifting between conceptual gestalts and, on the other, as a moral midget, committed primarily to the glorification of a particular narrative point of view rather than to the understanding of the empirical domain to which that narrative and others refer.[1]

[1] It is not generally appreciated how much the popularity of Kuhn among people in the humanities has been due to the satisfaction, sometimes glee, they take in what they see as his portrayal of the scientist as implicitly intellectually inferior to themselves. Your typical university literature lecturer, for example, thinks nothing of in a morning shifting through a whole range of gestalts (Marxist, Freudian, historical, New Criticism, deconstructionist, etc.) in interpreting a literary work.

For too long historical data from science have been collected, selected and interpreted mainly to answer questions posed by the various versions of the competing-theories narrative of scientific progress. The case for regarding this narrative as a general explanation of scientific advance has, in its various forms, been constructed primarily on the basis of examples drawn from physics. Yet even here on its most favoured ground it is a simple matter to show that the narrative of competing theories not only fails to account for but also runs counter to most major developments.

In physics today, indeed for a couple of generations now, fundamental research is focused primarily on "unification". Various schemes are used to characterize "the unification process", but all describe a state of affairs incomprehensible in terms of the traditional competing-theories narrative of scientific development. Stephen Hawking, for example, explains the quest as follows.

> "Today scientists describe the universe in terms of two basic partial theories – the general theory of relativity and quantum mechanics. They are the great intellectual achievements of the first half of this century. ... Unfortunately, however, these two theories are known to be inconsistent with each other – they cannot both be correct. One of the major endeavours in physics today... is the search for a new theory that will incorporate them both – a quantum theory of gravity" (Hawking 1995, p. 13).

Reading this passage through the competing-theories lens invites total misunderstanding. Physicists perceive relativity and quantum mechanics not as competing theories, but rather as different and complementing conceptual approaches to the fundamentals of physical reality. These two narratives illuminate separate facets of what unification physicists see as ultimately the same domain of inquiry, but which cannot yet be reconciled with each other. The unification dream, with its implicitly deeper level of understanding, *arises directly out of the co-existence of the two narratives*, the heuristic significance of each being enhanced by the existence of the other. Physicists seek neither to discredit relativity or quantum mechanics, but rather to create "a new theory that will incorporate them both".

Another and more common conceptualization of physics' unification project centres on the four forces of nature: gravity, electromagnetism, the weak nuclear force and the strong nuclear force. Physicists aim to develop a theory which merges the four forces into a single narrative scheme, or, as Hawking puts it, "to find a unified theory that will explain all four forces as different aspects of a single force" (p. 76). The theories of gravity, electromagnetism, and the two nuclear forces, as well as the theory of the electroweak force (a unification of the theories of electromagnetism and the weak nuclear force) are referred to as "partial" theories, because their frameworks of interpretation permit only partial and unreconciled views of the domain of force phenomena. *They are conceptually different ways of looking at that domain, and because they are conceptually different they reveal different dimensions of that domain.* Here again, as with electromagnetism, narrative pluralism is the indispensable prerequisite of fundamental scientific advance.

Shifting between narratives with fundamentally different conceptual systems can be a daily occurrence for 20th-century physicists. The time is long past when one could make a mark in theoretical physics without the ability to move freely between conceptual gestalts. Modern physics requires not only mathematical prowess but also conceptual agility. Unlike theory replacement, unification of narratives for a given domain demands the ability to jump back and forth between three or more conceptual systems: those of the incommensurate narratives and that of the narrative intended to effect the merger. But physicists working on unification projects are not alone in requiring conceptual ability. Today to become a physicist of any kind, one must master the basic concepts of both relativity and quantum mechanics. All the rest of modern physics is derived from one or the other of these two theories *whose conceptual frameworks differ radically*. Indeed "the basic concepts of relativity and quantum theory," notes David Bohm, "directly contradict each other" (Bohm 1983, p. 176).

> General relativity conceives of space and time as continuous; quantum theory conceives of them as discontinuous.

> General relativity conceives of matter as particulate; quantum theory conceives of it as a wave-particle duality.
>
> General relativity conceives of physical objects as having actual properties; quantum theory describes them as having only potential properties within the given physical situation.
>
> General relativity conceives all physical reality as determinate and all events as in principle having a causal explanation; quantum theory admits indeterminacy and events incapable of causal explanation.

Conceptual differences greater than these are scarcely imaginable. In their fundamentals, relativity and quantum theory share little in common as descriptive approaches to physical reality. Yet for most of a century these two metaphysically dissimilar narratives have worked not in competition but in tandem to the produce arguably the greatest advances in the history of science. And one simple fact has made this possible: *The primary commitment of the physics profession is not to narratives but to the advancement of knowledge.*

D. Anti-knowledge: four narrative pathologies

Robin Horton has categorized the similarities and differences between African traditional thought and western science. He identifies a general principle of divergence.

> "What I take to be the key difference is a very simple one. It is that in traditional cultures there is no developed awareness of alternatives to the established body of theoretical tenets; whereas in scientifically oriented cultures, such an awareness is highly developed. It is this difference we refer to when we say that traditional cultures are 'closed' and scientifically oriented cultures 'open'" (Horton 1971, p. 230).

A similar distinction pertains to communities of scholars and scientists associated with various domains of inquiry. Some are *open narrative communities*, in the sense that, *like modern physics*, they understand and support the epistemological importance of examining a domain from more than one narrative point of view. Others, like traditional societies, are *closed narrative communities* in that they insist that there is only one legitimate way of looking at their domain, all others being taboo. Open narrative communities may be the rule in the natural sciences, but in the human sciences they are few and far between. Closed narrative communities, however, rarely exist in isolation but rather in opposition to one or more other narrative communities focused on the same empirical domain. These oppositions do not create situations like those featured in the competing-theories narrative of scientific progress.

In the human sciences, narrative pluralism – far from being a normal state of affairs – rarely exists except as a temporary truce among mortal enemies. The conflict endemic to these less successful fields of formal inquiry is idiosyncratic and inadequately understood. The Popper/Kuhn narrative of scientific development contributes little to comprehending these domains, where theories "compete", but *not* in the traditional philosophy-of-science sense. Unlike natural scientists, social scientists never need to come up against reality's hard-edged recalcitrances. With rare exceptions, the links between social scientists narrative beliefs and the world around them are conceptually tenuous. Rarely do their domains generate significant falsifiable predictions, making it virtually unknown for a narrative community in the human sciences to reach the point where, in Kuhn's words, it "can no longer evade anomalies that subvert the existing tradition of scientific practice" (Kuhn 1970, p. 6). This freedom to forever evade reality when combined with monist beliefs and true-believer mentalities, leads to various narratives pathologies, of which four are especially important.

1. Narrative cleansing

Closed narrative communities typically live in open hostility toward "alien" narratives. There exists a danger of radically misunderstanding the basis of this belligerence. The despised narratives rather than being "competing" theories in the sense of the Popper/Kuhn story of scientific progress, are complementary theories in the sense of the narrative pluralism of 20th-century physics. Advocates of closed knowledge narratives often publicly embrace an extreme and primitive form of philosophical idealism, whereby they declare that their conceptual framework rather than offering a point of view on an empirical domain, determines the extent of that domain. This can be true even of narratives founded on a strictly materialist metaphysics. Behaviourist psychologists maintain that psychological phenomena not visible through their conceptual lens do not really exist. Horton describes a similar mind-set ("the magical world-view") common to traditional cultures.

> "Since he ['the traditional thinker'] can imagine no alternatives to his established system of concepts and words, the latter appear bound to reality in an absolute fashion. There is no way at all in which they can be seen as varying independently of the segments of reality they stand for. Hence they appear so integrally involved with their referents that any manipulation of the one self-evidently affects the other" (Horton 1971, p. 235).

Similarly, the behaviourist claim to universality entails that when it changes its conceptual framework, as it does from time to time, then the domain of psychological phenomena changes also. Those parts and aspects of the domain which cannot be perceived form the current conceptual point of view are said not to exist.

Knowledge narratives deployed hegemonically block or discourage other knowledge narratives and thereby the scrutiny of other aspects of reality. It can be said that this mode of narrative deployment constitutes *antiknowledge*. Consider a hypothetical example. The narrative called "Newtonian physics" could have been deployed (and perhaps was for a while) to block the study of elementary physical phenomena not covered by the Newtonian narrative, such as electro- electromagnetism and the two nuclear forces. Physicists could have retreated into subjective idealism and refused to recognize as "physical" those phenomena which cannot be embraced by the Newtonian narrative. They could have decreed that non-physical phenomena are precisely those phenomena that are incapable of being analyzed with the Newtonian narrative. This kind of radical inversion of the scientific ethos and retreat into ultra subjectivism is common place in the human sciences. For example, a standard economics graduate textbook informs its readers that "*noneconomic* problems are precisely those problems that are incapable of being analyzed with the *marginalist* paradigm" (Silberberg 1990, p.2). This mindset, which promotes and protects *a priori* thinking and is endemic to today's "mainstream" economics, anthropologists identify as characterizing traditional cultures. Their members, writes Evans-Pritchard, "reason excellently in the idiom of their beliefs, but they cannot reason outside, or against their beliefs because they have no other idiom in which to express their thoughts" (cited by Horton 1971, p. 231). This "absence of any awareness of alternatives" notes Horton, "makes for an absolute acceptance of the established theoretical tenets, and removes any possibility of questioning them" (p. 231).

Daniel Robinson, in his classic study of the history of psychology, describes an important example of anti-knowledge with a structure similar to the one noted by Harden in traditional cultures. Surveying the contemporary scene in American university psychology departments, Robinson notes that "hardly a vestige" remains of the program of experimental analysis of consciousness from earlier in the century.

> "But observe the difference between this shift in emphasis or complete abandonment of interest and the changes that have occurred in physics and biology. We *do* have minds, we *are* conscious, and we *can* reflect upon our private experiences because we *have* them. Unlike phlogiston or the inheritance of acquired characteristics, these phenomena exist and are the most common in human experience. The absence of orthodox Wundtians or Titchenerians or Jamesians, therefore, cannot be attributed to the disappearance of their subjects. Rather, it is to be understood as the result of the inability of the accepted *method* of psychological inquiry to address these subjects. The contemporary psychologist, if only insensibly, has made a *metaphysical* commitment to a method and has, per force, eliminated from the domain of significant issues those that

> cannot be embraced by that method" (Robinson 1986, p. 398).

Anyone coming from the natural sciences might wonder why social scientists expend so much time and energy "defining" and redefining their disciplines. But this otherwise pointless activity is a natural adjunct of anti-pluralism, it being an easy shortcut to narrative cleansing. The anti-pluralist seeks to establish as off-limits those areas and aspects of the empirical domain not visible from his or her single chosen conceptual vantage point. *Laying down a definition which excludes phenomena invisible through that system, works to establish a professional taboo against the extension of human knowledge and understanding to all the rest of that empirical domain.* This technique of defining away the unwanted is common to many forms of anti-pluralism. Two notorious examples are the Nazis defining "German" so as to exclude Germans who were Jewish, and America's founding fathers defining "citizen" so to as to exclude Americans of African descent.

A movement that began on the fringes of economics in the 1990s illustrates points raised in this section. The history of economics is diverse but nevertheless anathema to the idea of pluralism. Beginning with the French Physiocrates in the mid 18th-century, economists of all varieties have been inclined to believe that their approach to economic phenomena reveals, if not the whole truth, at least all of it that is worth knowing. It is with these broad conceptualizations, which are called "schools", rather than with subject areas, that economists, like psychologists, form their primary professional identity. The assorted teachings and members of these narrative schools are labelled orthodox or heterodox depending on whether their school is the dominate one or not. Until very recently economists of all varieties have been comfortable with this quasi theological scheme of things.

But from the 1960s on, neoclassical economists were increasingly successful at purging economics departments of economists who viewed economic reality through other conceptual lenses. This cleansing took place worldwide, a process that accelerated with the rise of neoliberalism, which justifies itself by appeal to the Neoclassical narrative.

Traditionally non-Neoclassical schools of economics have quarrelled among themselves hardly less than with the Neoclassical. But in the mid-nineties, faced with near extinction, a peace movement began among these schools. Under the banner ICARE (Confederation of Associations for the Reform of Economics) (later changed to ICAPE, with "Pluralism" substituted for "Reform") it sought, declared its manifesto, "to promote a new spirit of pluralism in economics, involving critical conversation and tolerant communication among different approaches". But as these words show, this is a pluralism in the mode of a council of churches, a strategic pluralism *rather than the epistemological pluralism of the natural sciences* that this book endorses. Even so, ICAPE's conciliation campaign helped to breakdown among non-Neoclassical economists the Popperian-Kuhnian tradition of viewing economics through the lens of competing narratives. This proved to be prophetic. In the summer of 2000 a group of French economics students circulated a petition that attracted attention from the media in France and subsequently from economists worldwide. The students labelled mainstream economics "autistic" because its allegiance to a single narrative necessarily means that in the main it refuses to look at economic reality. The students called for "a plurality of approaches adapted to the complexity of objects analyzed."

Their small but skilfully focused rebellion against economics' traditional quasi-religious approach led to the emergence of the Real-World Economics movement, including the establishment of the World Economics Association whose manifesto unreservedly embraces the narrative pluralism of the natural sciences.

2. Fake pluralism

As a means of fending off criticism of its autism, of further concealing its ideological role (see below), of diverting calls for pluralism and, perhaps most of all, just as a pastime, economics' Neoclassical mainstream plays a game of relaxing the assumptions. It loosens one or two assumptions around the edges of the theory and then does a bit of analysis. This is no better than when viewing *David* to lean to the left or to the right or kneel or stand tiptoed as a means of seeing another side of Michelangelo's masterpiece. Yet the whole mainstream project is now so infected with this methodological dilettantism that it seems necessary to spell out the difference between fake and real pluralism.

Even more than with a word, the meaning of a concept is it use. The meaning of a word depends upon the referent of the sentence, which as Wittgenstein noted is a "state of affairs" (*Tractatus Logico-Philosophicus* 2.01, 2.001, 2.02); likewise the meaning of a concept depends on the framework in which it appears. For example, take something so simple and straightforward as the concept of economic growth defined in terms of Gross National Product. When you transfer this concept from the Neoclassical framework which views the economy as a closed system that includes the ecosystem ("land, labour and capital") to the conceptual framework of ecological economics which views the economy as an open subsystem of the ecosystem, this concept's meaning, in all its dimensions, changes fundamentally. It also changes fundamentally when transferred from the masculinist Neoclassical framework to a feminist economics that ascribes economic value to production not entering into market relations, for example family-provided nursing and child care. Each of these three conceptual frameworks, having the limited point of view common to all such creations, identify and describe a different "state of affairs". These examples illustrate two fundamental points: One must think from *inside* a conceptual system in order to:

1. grasp the meaning of its concepts and
2. gain the vantage point that it offers on the world.

It is only when you shift from one conceptual system to another, *like physicists do*, not when you relax some assumptions of one system, that you have real pluralism.

3. Narrative inversion

A knowledge narrative may become *invert*, meaning that instead of being used mainly as an instrument for explaining reality, its focus becomes itself. Turning away from the empirical phenomena that inspired it, it becomes transfixed with its own existence. This may take the form of formalism, where the narrative's empirical content is subordinated to the articulation of formal devices, where a language "refers to the observer's logic but not to the subject" (Piaget 1973, p. 25), as in much recent economics and political science, or with an obsessive hermeneutic interest in "reading" and interpreting the formative texts of the narrative, theology being the supreme example, but with psychoanalysis sometimes not far behind.

In subject areas where experimentation is difficult or impossible, mathematical models may have no connection with the concrete or empirical world. Symbols in the equations, instead of referring to measurable quantities, may be only imaginary placeholders, like "Monopoly money" is imaginary money. In these cases – and they are especially common in economics – the models are merely play things, "being no more than a play of mathematical relations" (Piaget 1973, p. 25), referring only to those relations themselves, rather than to relations in the empirical world. The practitioners are not "engaged in forging tools to arrange and measure actual facts so much as making a marvellous array of pretend-tools which would perform wonders if ever a set of facts should turn up in the right form" (Worswick 1972, p. 79). In economics the inversion often goes even further. There exist branches of economics that differ from branches of mathematics only in two respects: they are of no real mathematical interest and some of their axioms and terminology may have in the distant past been related to some empirical question. In these pursuits, so favoured by promotion and grant- and prize-giving committees, further assumptions are made willy-nilly to facilitate mathematical manipulation rather than from any desire to simulate reality. And by varying the empirically empty assumptions, thereby generating an endless range of conceivable logical possibilities, a virtual infinity of "models" can be fabricated, each generating one or more publications and all impregnable to empirical critique – a scientist's nightmare, but a careerist's dream.

4. Concealed ideologies

A conceptual system defines, at the exclusion of others, a point of view toward its object of enquiry. For the human sciences this fact poses a moral danger. Their conceptual systems relate to their objects of enquiry in two ways that invite them to play an ideological function as well as an epistemological one. Both of these relations are recursive. First, a social-science conceptual system can alter the objects of its enquiry by becoming part of the conceptual and belief apparatus through which humans define themselves, perceive others and make choices, thereby changing the structures and propensities of the human world. With the spread of mass higher education, these recursive phenomena become more common, pervasive and profound. Second, unlike the natural sciences, the human sciences are ultimately a means from on high of preserving or reconstructing the basic realities that they study, these in total being the human project. Different conceptual systems present different sets of choices, real or imagined, to be chosen and acted upon by human populations at large. It can never be the case that each of these sets of choices will equally favour every group in society.

This means that, regardless of value judgments, it is the nature of all social theorizing, economics being no exception, to favour some groups in society over others, so that any attempt to block enquiry and analysis from multiple theoretical perspectives, i.e., anti-pluralism, is an ideological move.

Since Napoleon's popularisation of "ideology" in a derogative sense, many commentators have attached various meanings to the word, meanings inspired partly by shifting historical and social contexts, partly by a desire to make the phenomenon intelligible from more than one conceptual viewpoint and partly also, of course, by ideology. But the common presumption of these formulations has been that an ideology is necessarily manufactured and/or disseminated, consciously or unconsciously, with an ideological end in mind. The presumption of intent holds not only for the concept as developed in the negative sense by Marxist and non-Marxist writers, but also for Mannheim's neutralized concept which identifies ideology as a distinct type of cultural formation, functionally indispensable in non-traditional societies. But the preceding taxonomy of differences in conceptual systems shows that the element of intent is not a necessary condition for an economic theory to function as an ideology. Each conceptual system for a given human field necessarily offers a different viewpoint of that field, and thereby suggests different possibilities for shaping, directing and organizing it. Consequently, if for whatever reasons, one conceptual system's partial view is made the only view on offer, its influence on shaping human experience in a particular direction will be no less than if it had been designed to do so. *Where there exist a plurality of conceptual systems that illuminate different dimensions of a social object but the teaching of only one system is permitted, that system functions as an ideology.*

One must be careful here not to fall into a logical hole. Because every possible conceptual system can view its social object only from a particular point of view, it is self-defeating to equate ideology with systematized bias *vis-à-vis* the social realm, lest the social sciences are to be regarded as but a subcategory of ideology. The test of whether or not an economic theory is ideological is not its essence nor how and through whom it came to be nor who uses it. Instead the test is *how* it is used. A knife can be a deadly weapon or a tool for preparing the family dinner. Likewise an approach to economics can be an exercise in ideology or a tool for the advancement of understanding. A conceptual system regarding human affairs becomes an ideology when its partisans refuse to countenance the use of other systems as well, as when a group of economists refuse to teach their students how to view the economic realm from conceptual points of view other than the one that they favour. It is important to note here how the epistemological and ideological dimensions relate. *An economic theory becomes an ideology precisely at that moment when its partisans decide to curb the growth and prevent the dissemination of knowledge of how to see all those aspects of the economy that their approach leaves in the dark.* In economics ideology comes about mostly through the way it is taught, so that the primary agents of ideology in economics are not theorists and technical practitioners, but rather the teachers and, most especially, the authors of textbooks. In Chapter 3 we will look more closely at how in the social sciences ideology, ethics and epistemology are inextricably interconnected.

E. Summing up

Even more than physics, modern medicine, where the general practitioner shifts freely between knowledge narratives, exemplifies the antithesis of the monistic approach to knowledge that characterizes traditional societies and many human sciences. The germ theory of disease, along with psychosomatic, genetic and life-style explanations of disease are narratives between which the competent doctor shifts freely back and forth in seeking a true and full explanation of his or her patient's complaint. These narratives have overlapping domains – for example, diet (not enough red wine and too much butter) and stress (not enough leisure and too much aggro) contributing through bio-chemical processes to genetic susceptibility to heart disease. But there is no yearning or pressure in the community of medicine for a reduction of its many knowledge narratives to a master narrative, nor for a unification of narratives as in physics. Instead the medical community understands that its multiplicity of narratives for explaining disease and its absence is needed to serve *the complexity of medicine's empirical domain*. Indeed, it is almost self-evident that the ill-health and good-health of the human organism are causally more complex that the fundamental properties of the physical universe, and, therefore, not open to narrative unification. It should be self-evident that this is even truer of the socio-economic realm.

If the human sciences are to be a constructive part of the human conversation, they must be willing to adjust the conceptual vantage points of their narratives both to fit changes in the topics of that conversation through time and to illuminate the diverse perspectives of its participants. Above all, the conceit that because one is a social scientist one is blessed with a privileged or God's-eye view of the human world must not be indulged. Richard Rorty's injunction to philosophers is no less apt for social scientists: "to be rational is to be willing to refrain from... thinking that there is a special set of terms in which all contributions to the conversation should be put – and to be willing to pick up the jargon of the interlocutor rather than translating it into one's own" (Rorty 1980, p. 318). Epistemologically this is the recognition that a plurality of narratives enriches our understanding of any sub-domain of the human project, that, whereas in the special case such narratives may be incompatible, in general they are complimentary and their plurality essential to the advancement of knowledge and the good health of society.

Chapter 2

Intersubjective reality, intrasubjective theory

The idea of intersubjectivity is the hypothesis that human consciousnesses are constitutionally interdependent, that, as unique human personalities, we form and reform ourselves, not in isolation, but rather in relation to and under the influence of other human subjects and institutions. Neither now nor in other recent eras is this a view likely to provoke wide controversy. So it is markedly strange that intersubjectivity, under any name, did not figure significantly in modern philosophy until the last century, did not until recently mediate in social theory between holistic and radically individualistic explanations, and to this day remains axiomatically banished from a Neoclassical mainstream narrative founded on subjective value theory.[1]

The origins of this banishment seem incompletely understood. Much has been written about how the desire to model economics after classical mechanics required the assumption of economic agents whose individual identities, like Newton's atoms, are unchanging and, most especially, impervious to mutual influence (Mirowski 1989; Fullbrook 1996; 1997). But from where did this unlikely idea about human beings come? And why, when it runs contrary to all known experience, have so many intelligent and educated people found it plausible? Does a philosophically grounded intersubjective alternative exist? Finding the answers to these questions is a prerequisite for advancing economics beyond the reign of the Neoclassical model of *homo economicus*. This chapter looks for answers in the histories of modern philosophy and social theory and their relations to economics. What follows is divided into three sections. The first explores the tradition of Western intrasubjective philosophy, the second traces the development of intersubjective philosophy and social theory – especially African-American

[1] There is of course also "intersubjectivity" in the modern epistemological and procedural sense of the testing of hypothesizes.

thought – and the third, in the light of the first two, considers the strange case of economics.

Intrasubjective philosophy

Prior to the Enlightenment, most people enjoyed religious certainty regarding their notion of self and of their place in the world. But from the Sixteenth Century onward, secularized conceptions undermined religious ones, depriving the latter of their self-evident status, and so destroying the certainty regarding self that had been a common birthright in the West for centuries. René Descartes [1696-1650] began his famous metaphysical deliberations (*Discourse on Method*, 1637; *Mediations*, 1641) at this historical crossroads. Plagued by existential despair – he felt that even his own existence fell within "the sphere of the doubtful" – the French philosopher resolved to overcome it by rediscovering – he knew not yet where – certainty.

For this quest Descartes invented a method which he explains as follows:

> "I thought it necessary ... to reject as if utterly false anything in which I could discover the least grounds for doubt, so that I could find out if I was left with anything at all which was absolutely indubitable" (*Discourse on Method*, part IV).

Descartes counted as doubtable anything revealed by our senses, because sometimes they deceive us (as when a straight stick looks bent in water).

> "...how do I know that He [an all-powerful God] has not brought it to pass that there is no earth, no heaven, no extended body, no magnitude, no place, and that nevertheless they seem to me to exist just exactly as I now see them" (First Meditation, p. 18).

Descartes concluded that he did not and could not know these things for certain. Furthermore, this uncertainty and his methodological doubt extended to the existence of his own body.

> "I shall consider myself as having no hands, no eyes, no flesh, no blood, nor any senses, yet falsely believing myself to possess all these things... (First Meditation, Haldane and Ross, p. 19).

Having a body, Descartes concluded, was not part of his essential nature. In the end only his existence as an incorporeal thinking being withstood his program of radical doubt. "I am thinking, therefore I exist." On the basis of this alleged disembodied subjective certainty, together with an argument for a perfect God, Descartes sought to re-establish "objective" knowledge. That he succeeded is debatable. What is not is that his presumption of subjective certainty became the foundation of modern philosophy.

Descartes may only have been seeking a way beyond an existential and epistemological impasse. But his solution offered a new conception of the human self, one that, in the centuries that followed, permeated, defined and structured intellectual pursuits including philosophy, social theory and economics, and, through these, shaped the thinking of the general populations of Western societies. By conceiving himself as disembodied, Descartes not only found the metaphysical certainty that he desired, but also initiated the idea of a thinker/observer who is completely detached, existing independently of time, place and other human beings, and therefore, like God, totally objective. "I am a substance", he wrote in A *Discourse on Method* (Part IV),

> "the whole nature or essence of which is to think, and which for its existence does not need any place or depend on any material thing."

This phantom of perfect self-consciousness and independence was reified by succeeding generations to become the intellectual ideal of Western society, an ideal that academics came increasingly to believe they had attained.

British empiricism, contrary sometimes to popular belief, founded itself on Descartes' notion of a completely autonomous self, separate from place, time, materiality and society, and therefore self-identical over time. True,

John Locke [1632-1704] broke with Rationalism by declaring that all our ideas were derived from experience (*An Essay Concerning Human Understanding*, 1690). But he saw knowledge as a product of reason working out the connections between those ideas, and he insisted upon Descartes' phantom as the agent who carries out this process of reason. Locke made a distinction between "person" and "man", and, by extension, between personal identity and a man's identity. The identity of a *man*, he wrote, is

> "participation of the same continued life, by constantly fleeting particles of matter, in succession vitally united to the same organized body" (*An Essay Concerning Human Understanding* II. xxvii, 6).

But the identity of a *person* is that of

> "a thinking intelligent being, that has reason, and reflection, and can consider itself as itself, the same thinking thing in different times and places" (II. xxvii. 9).

Locke's thinker is not his concept of "man" but rather his Cartesian concept of "person", who, out of ideas, creates knowledge independently of time, place and society, and who became for British philosophers, no less than for Continentals, their imaginary ideal persona.

At times the Scottish philosopher David Hume [1711-1777] courted scandal by rejecting the notion that we know ourselves as simple, unified beings who are self-identical from one time to another. He offered his famous metaphor of the theatre and suggested that each of us

> "is nothing but a bundle or collection of different perceptions, which succeed each other with an inconceivable rapidity, and are in a perpetual flux and movement" (*A Treatise of Human Nature*, 1739-40, Book I, section VI).

But this outlook, so unflattering to members of his profession, failed to seduce them. Indeed, following the appearance of Immanuel Kant's *Critique of Pure Reason* (1781), Hume's unassuming assessment of the nature of a philosopher's self disappeared from sight. By identifying Descartes' disembodied God-like self with philosophers in particular, Kant offered his colleagues a view of themselves that too few since have been able to resist. He sought to show that philosophical knowledge can transcend the bounds of experience, and this required him to center the putative power of transcendence with philosophers themselves.

Through the centuries the inward-looking line philosophical narrative begun by Descartes became a worldly and pervasive narrative in society. The Cartesian view of human reality, both on the Continent and in Britain, shaped the way we think, especially the way we theorize, about all aspects of social and personal existence, including, as we shall see, the economic. Descartes' disembodiment of the thinker created a conceptually unbridgeable gap between the observer and the observed, the knower and the known, the subject and the object, thereby ascribing to each individual two separate planes of existence, an inside and an outside: one where we are the observer, the knower and the subject, the other where we are the observed, the known and the object of thought and perception. Under this dualism the body came to be thought of as a mere capsule, with windows called sense organs, in which human consciousness, cut off from the immediacy of the world around it and forever secure from the possibility of intersubjectivity, lived. This led to the tradition of thinking of the "nature" of human beings abstractly, as outside and beyond society, thereby erasing the complex and ongoing development of human agents.

In some spheres the categorical denial of intersubjectivity continued through the Twentieth Century. Indeed, with the advent of the Analytical movement, Descartes' disembodied philosopher reached new heights of godliness. Bertrand Russell, in *The Problems of Philosophy* (1912), effectively the movement's manifesto, first sets out the agenda, then calls for the development of philosophers capable of realizing it. The job specifications do not fit everyone. For recruits, Russell wants only intellects capable of "true philosophic contemplation" who:

> "will see as God might see, without a *here* and *now*, without hopes and fears, without the trammels of customary beliefs

> and traditional prejudices, calmly, dispassionately, in the sole and exclusive desire of knowledge – knowledge as impersonal, as purely contemplative, as it is possible for man to attain. Hence also the free intellect will value more the abstract and universal knowledge into which the accidents of private history do not enter, than the knowledge brought by the senses, and dependent, as such knowledge must be, upon an exclusive and personal point of view and a body whose sense-organs distort as much as they reveal" (Russell [1912]1967, p. 93)

Faith in this atemporal, disembodied and, therefore, intrasubjective self, both as an ultimate unit of analysis and as constituting the accredited performing philosopher, underwrites the analytical tradition. It is especially conspicuous in the tradition's considerations of "rationality", as when John Rawls reveals the foundational presuppositions of his celebrated *A Theory of Justice* (1971).

> The essential point is that we need an argument showing which principles, if any, free and equal rational persons would choose... My suggestion is that we think of the original position as the point of view from which noumenal selves see the world... The description of the original position interprets the point of view of the noumenal selves,... (Rawls 1971, pp. 255-6).

For philosophers, this notion that some individuals possess the means to "see as God might see", to attain "the original position" so that their point of view should then outweigh and invalidate all others holds a powerful attraction, capable of seducing the best minds, even Bertrand Russell's.

Intersubjective philosophy and social theory

At the beginning of the 19th century, Georg Hegel [1770-1831] rebelled against the abstract universalism of the Enlightenment by turning the Cartesian subjective self inside-out. He argued that history displays a determinate direction and process of development, powered by an evolving collective Mind of which individual minds are but the finite and historically determined parts. Hegel's works include brilliant analyses of how individual consciousnesses depend on recognition from others and of how they are socially constructed, and also of how reason is a changing structure of consciousness rather than an eternal archetype. In the main, however, Hegel's philosophy dissolves subjectivity into a collective whole. Under his system, individual subjects are not so much "inter" related as "sub" related to an historical, all-transcending and largely determinate totality. This, as explanation, reverses the direction of causation. Just as the atomistic Cartesian self underpins methodological individualism, the "Hegelian self", and its related notion of an all-encompassing whole, provides the ontological foundation of methodological holism. For the realm of human affairs, Hegel, in effect, reversed the putative direction of causality between the whole and the parts.

Intersubjective philosophy, which, in its modern from, emerged only in the last century, occupies the ambiguous middle-ground between these Cartesian and Hegelian extremes. It conceives of the individual as neither wholly autonomous nor wholly dependent, as neither wholly closed nor wholly open. This intrinsic conceptual ambiguity of the intersubjective project accounts in part for its failure to develop as a well-defined philosophical movement. Unlike its atomistic and holistic rivals, intersubjective philosophy, including its social theory offshoots, does not have categorical certainty at its command with which to frame pontifical pronouncements. Even its origins, though recent, are obscure and a little confusing.

Although the phenomenological movement, as founded by the German philosopher Edmund Husserl [1859-1938] at the beginning of the last century, is generally recognized as the watershed in the growth of the intersubjective approach to philosophy, the crucial philosophical moves that made it possible date from the late 1900s. The first involved dusting off an old idea, one common to the Scholastics of the Middle Ages. Philosophers had not always believed that consciousness was a container in which a person could, like Descartes, find the their virgin self lurking in some obscure interior corner, or, like *homo economicus*, observe their inner self to discover the data needed to construct their consumer preference map. Descartes' sharp separation of body and mind led inevitably to the distinction between external and inner perception (or Locke's "sensation" and "reflection") which, in turn, required the notion of consciousness as a space where things exist through time and can be inventoried and measured by some further entity that is never named. Today this 17th-century notion of consciousness remains, alas, the sole version of the truth in most of the world's Economics departments. But in 1870s Vienna a very different notion of consciousness was advanced, one that conceives of consciousness not as a repository but as a relation. This is Franz Brentano's theory of intentionality (1874).

Brentano's theory states that consciousness is always consciousness *of* something. Instead of regarding consciousness as a kind of receptacle holding perceptions, sense data and images, Brentano taught – and his students included Franz Kafka, Carl Stumpf, Sigmund Freud, Alexius Meinong, Christain von Ehrenfels, Edmund Husserl, Bertrand Russell, G. E. Moore, Max Scheler and Martin Heidegger – that consciousness is a *relation* that human beings have to objects, material and immaterial, including those real, imagined and remembered (Honderich 1995, p. 104). Every moment of consciousness has something *of which* it is conscious. Brentano's conception of consciousness as a relation that a being has to other beings and kinds of being, rather than a separate area of being, renders nonsensical attempts to look inwards for the self or ego or, indeed, for consumer preferences. Instead this view implies that the self – or selves – is, like everything else known in the world, merely an object *of* consciousness and thus, given the flow of consciousness, *continually open to reconstruction*.

Brentano's principle of intentionality has a further dimension disruptive of the traditional metaphysical order. It maintains that it is the objects themselves – the Coca Cola bottle, the bowl of chili, the juicy red apple – which figure in acts of consciousness. This view contravenes philosophy's empirical tradition, as well as the Cartesian branch of the continental tradition, which, as in Hume's theatre analogy, tends to regard consciousness as an indirect and passive experience of the world. It is indirect because it holds that when one looks at the red apple, the actual apple is not the object of consciousness, but rather a likeness or picture of the apple which appears *in* one's consciousness. Thus, this view regards perception as only indirectly of things in the world. The principle of intentionality changes all that. The redness and juiciness of the apple are no longer "sensations" but rather what is sensed; they are properties of the apple which consciousness intends, rather than elements of consciousness representative of those properties. Under this narrative, the world is seen as something through which a consciousness moves and intervenes, and interacts and transmutes with other consciousnesses and their creations.

The other great demolisher of the Cartesian myth of a stable, coherent, disembodied and atomistic self, and the person whom Edmund Husserl credited as "the father of phenomenology", was Henri Bergson. Whereas Brentano focused on the nature of consciousness *vis-à-vis* the world, Bergson explored its and the self's relation to time and to the body. Today Bergson appears as a paradoxical figure in the history of philosophy. Although little read in the last seventy years (notwithstanding his recent revival), he has had immense influence, having been widely read, discussed and digested by other philosophers in his own lifetime [1859–1941].

Bergson's ontological world differed fundamentally from his predecessors. His philosophical interest was in Becoming rather than Being and in concrete particulars rather than in abstract and universal forms. These philosophical predilections made for great and productive mischief when applied to the notion of the human subject. Although Bergson conceived of the self as unified, he attributed this property not to the existence of a continuing essence, but to an evolving life-history that could accommodate change in all aspects of one's personal identity. He emphasized the openness of the human subject, its developmental nature and its possibility of indeterminate – that is, real – choice. By working on the plane of living reality, Bergson deconstructed the stable and determinant self so loved by philosophers.

But Bergson's demolition of the Cartesian self went much further. He also escaped from the traditional mind/body dualism, and did so without resorting to reductive materialism. The following brief passage, in which the perceptions and actions referred to are his own, encapsulates his central innovation.

> "... thus perceptions are born and actions made ready. *My body* is that which stands out as the center of the perceptions; *my personality* is the being to which these actions must be referred" (Bergson [1896]1991, p. 47).

Rather than regarding his body as something distinct from his self or "personality", his body *is* him in so far as he is an active person. His body is the "center" of the perceptions on the basis of which he chooses his bodily actions which, in turn, refer back to his self. His body, far from belonging to a distinct realm of being, is central to and inseparable from how he experiences himself and how he chooses himself. In short, his self is *embodied*. This placement of the subject visibly and vulnerably in-the-world, when coupled with the intentionality principle, gave rise to the notion of intersubjectivity.

Edmund Husserl brought together these advances by Brentano and Bergson and made "intersubjectivity" part of the philosopher's lexicon. He recognized that for each of us the phenomenological status of the world is a reality shared with other human subjects. We are each integrally linked or embedded in this social reality, and the linkage is dynamic and diverse. Let me elaborate.

The mind's embodiment means that the self exists "out there" as a natural and social entity, intersubjectively permeable and therefore only partially under our control. Daily existence brings us in contact with the Other, both individual and collective others who apprehend our bodies and our personas from perspectives different from our own. Thus, to comprehend one's self as a worldly subject/object one needs to adopt the multifarious and shifting perspectives of others. Furthermore, all our social acts (and very few of our acts are not social) take place in preexisting and ever-changing fields of intersubjective meaning. Events are, wrote Husserl, "experienced by each perceiving subject in a preconstituted intersubjective field of experience, events in which several human subjects participate" (quoted in Petit 1999, p. 233) Our experiences, including those formative and reformative of our individual selves, take place *inside intersubjective structures* – genders, races, languages, legends, histories, governments, fashions, genres, games, news, professions, families, romances, friendships, etc., etc. – which we, as autonomous individuals, may modify but which are ontological prior to each of our individual subjectivities, selves, preferences, etc.. Nor do the complications of intersubjectivity for the constitution of our selves stop here. Our social embeddedness is kaleidoscopic. In the coming and going of everyday life, as well as in the pursuit of ambitions, we enter and leave, and simultaneously inhabit different intersubjective fields, micro and macro, and with diverse and changing sets of people, which exercise their different influences on who we are. Finally, the view that intersubjective consciousness is built into selfhood, that intersubjectivity is an integral aspect of the self as subject, means that the we-dimension is ontologically fundamental to human reality.

This broadly intersubjective conception of the human being, *the intersubjective self,* that emerged in twentieth-century philosophy carries us a very long way from Descartes' notion of consciousness as a private and impenetrable walled-off sphere, wherein resides a pristine self that commands the certainty of definition and constancy through time to support the God-like vision of Russell, the linguistic atomism of the early Wittgenstein, the noumenal self of Rawls and the well-defined and stable preferences of the Neoclassical economist.

The intersubjective alternative to the Enlightenment's Cartesian subject moved philosophy out of the realm of pure logic and pure thought by linking it to the physical, social and cultural worlds, including the general flux of experience. As always with revolutions, this one had unintended and unanticipated consequences, the most important being that it provided the first adequate philosophical grounding for social theory.

It was no longer necessary for philosophical-grounded non-holistic social theory to regard human "nature" as outside or before society or a-historical and static. Instead the human subject was now conceived of as intrinsically ambiguous and variable, each individual uniquely situated or embedded in an ever-changing intersubjective world, partly self-defined, partly defined by their history of particular situations. According to intersubjective philosophy, writes Mark Poster:

> "Not only did the individual inject meaning into the world, but the world injected meaning into the individual, so that the individual was immediately social. Defined both by others and by himself, he was out there in the world, perceiving and being perceived through his body" (Poster 1975, p. 148).

Of course, all this is only commonsense. But, as I have shown, it is a way of seeing the human world that completely contradicts the philosophical tradition set in motion by the Enlightenment. The *intersubjective self* stands far removed from the idea of the single and unified self or subject presupposed by analytical philosophy and Neoclassical economics. Under the new way of thinking, one's view of oneself is neither more real than nor exempt from the influence of the views that others hold of oneself. Rather than being a simple and given unity, or even a unity formed on the basis of logical entailment, one's self is a synthesis requiring management, upkeep, investment, friends, perhaps even therapy.

Through phenomenology, the post-Cartesian and post-Hegelian upsurge established the irreducibility of intersubjective consciousness, and thereby the joint interdependence of the "I" and the "We", of the individual and society, of the event and history, rather than the dependence of one on the other that theretofore had in the main characterized social philosophy and social theory. This re-conceptualization of the human being was potentially momentous to the human sciences, including economics. This is because every study or narrative of human behavior bases itself, explicitly or implicitly, on some conception or model of the human being, which then determines the scope, nature and often the conclusions of its inquiry. Intellectuals did not take long to see that the intersubjective perspective had the effect of opening up new frontiers of the phenomenal world to investigation and perhaps even to understanding. From the 1930s on, the influence of the intersubjective conceptual foundation spread through social thought in numerous directions. These included French Existentialism (especially Simone de Beauvoir, Maurice Merleau-Ponty, and Jean-Paul Sartre), European and American sociology, (first Max Scheler, Karl Mannheim and Alfred Schutz, later Norbert Elias, Erving Goffman, Maurice Natanson, Thomas Luckmann, Perter Berger and Pierre Bourdieu), ethnomethodology (Harold Garfinkel), psychiatry (R.D. Laing), the many-faceted Frankfurt School (especially Walter Benjamin, Max Horkheimer, Erich Fromm and Jurgen Habermas), and, of course, the later work of Ludwig Wittgenstein and his followers, which showed that intersubjective, not intrasubjective, experience is the foundation of language.

This account of the development of intersubjective social theory remains radically incomplete. There is another side, one pioneered by women and people of colour that is no less important, although traditionally, alas, omitted from accounts such as this one. Both atomistic and holistic social theories leave oppressed social/cultural groups out in the cold. Atomistic theory tells the oppressed that their predicament is their own fault, and holistic theory that it is due to macro forces beyond their influence. So for such groups to launch, prior to the developments described above, liberation movements grounded in social theory, they themselves had to intellectually pioneer a way though the intersubjective middle, one that included both upward and downward causation (social structures shaped by individuals and vice a versa), one that emphasized the social construction of individuals but also taught them both how to collectively reconstruct themselves as individuals and how to band together to manipulate and change macro forces and structures.

African-American social thought and a celebrated economist

Whereas today academic social theory is predominately concerned with traditional white male reality – social class, socio-economic status and occupational ranking – it used to be exclusively so. But for social theorists who belonged to oppressed groups and who in consequence usually found themselves outside the academy, oppression was the central issue. It fell to them to theorize the relations between the races and between the sexes. Indeed, it was these men and women who linked social theory to questions of human emancipation and developed the intersubjective social analysis, especially intersubjective identity theory, that broke down the traditional "division between conceptions of the person and conceptions of people in society" (Elias 1978, p. 129), and that increasingly underpins today's academic sociology.

Olympe de Gouges in France (*The Declaration of the Rights of Woman and the Female Citizen*, 1791) and Mary Wollstonecraft in England (*A Vindication of the Rights of Woman*, 1792) argued that women were socially constructed according to cultural notions of "feminine" and that these structures could and should be changed. De Gouges paid the ultimate price for her cultural heresy and died on the guillotine. But her and Wollstonecraft's ideas were amplified at the women's rights convention held at Seneca Falls, New York, USA in 1848. Symbiotically, this important event coincided with the rise of the American anti-slavery movement. In 1845 Frederick Douglass, escaped slave and intellectual, published his influential autobiography with its narrative structured around the idea that observable differences between the races and the identities of their members are socially and economically constructed rather than natural or innate or intrasubjective.

By the end of the 19th century these intersubjective ideas were central to a growing body of African-American social thought, most notably in the work of the sociologist W. E. B. Du Bois. In 1903 Du Bois, who had studied under William James at Harvard and later at the University of Berlin, published *The Souls of Black Folk*. It includes a short passage that has been quoted hundreds if not thousands of times and that I am going to quote again because it has been so influential in the development of contemporary social theory. The African-American, writes Du Bois, lives in:

> "... a world which yields him no true self-consciousness, but only lets him see himself through the revelation of the other world. It is a peculiar sensation this double consciousness, this sense of always looking at one's self though the eyes of others, of measuring one's soul by the tape of a world that looks on in amused contempt and pity. One ever feels his twoness, -- an American, A Negro; two souls, two thoughts, two unreconciled strivings; two warring ideals in one dark body, ..." (Du Bois [1903]1965, pp. 214-5).

Here, in a few words, Du Bois harnesses together a formidable and formative team of intersubjective concepts:

- the self permeated by the social world,

- the social construction of race,
- the social embeddedness of the individual self,
- embeddedness in contradictory positions resulting in multiple selves or identities,
- the subject-object dichotomy in social relations,
- embodiment and, of course,
- the Other.

But what does this have to do with economics? Well, consider Du Bois's next paragraph where he applies some of these concepts to understanding a situation of "two unreconciled strivings".

> "The history of the American Negro is the history of strife, – this longing to attain self-conscious manhood, to merge his double self into a better and true self. In this merging he wishes neither of the older selves to be lost. He would not Africanize America, for America has too much to teach the world and Africa. He would not bleach his Negro soul in a flood of white Americanism, for he knows that Negro blood has a message for the world. He simply wishes to make it possible for a man to be both a Negro and an American, without being cursed and spit upon by his fellows, without having the doors of Opportunity closed roughly in his face" (Du Bois [1903]1965, p. 215).

But our perceptions of economic phenomena have become so conditioned by neoclassicism that the penny may still not have dropped. So consider yet another passage, this one first published in 2002 and whose author and source I will for the moment withhold.

> "... dispossessed races and classes face a Hobbesian choice. One possibility is to choose an identity that adapts to the dominant culture. But such an identity is adopted with the knowledge that full acceptance by members of the dominant culture is unlikely. Such a choice is also likely to be psychologically costly to oneself since it involves being someone "different"; family and friends, who are also outside

> the dominant culture are likely also to have negative attitudes toward a maverick who has adopted it. Thus individuals are likely to feel that they can never fully 'pass'."

In the paragraph following this passage its author cites Du Bois's *The Souls of Black Folk*, but, unfortunately, without suggesting any direct indebtedness. The author is George Akerlof, winner in 2001 of what is popularly known as the Nobel Prize for Economics, and the passage quoted is from the paper he delivered when accepting the prize (Akerlof 2002, p. 427).

Economics

Akerlof has sought to show the role that intersubjectively determined group identities play in the distribution of income and in the shaping of economic agents. This project deserves every possible encouragement, but it is very far from being based on a new idea. A central thesis of Simone de Beauvoir's *The Second Sex* and of the materialist school of feminism (Christine Delphy, Colette Guillaumin, Monique Wittig, Ann Oakley, ...) is that gender derives in large part from economic relations, especially divisions of labor by sex, not only between occupations, but also between paid and unpaid labor. This feminist argument is an application of the older and more general hypothesis that situations of work, including training for them, entail intersubjective effects that radically shape and reshape individual and groups of workers. A century of Neoclassical hegemony seems to have erased from the profession's memory the fact that this hypothesis stood at the origins of modern economics and was fundamental to Adam Smith's "principle of division of labour". It is worth quoting Smith at length, if only to show that economists, in the beginning, neither denied intersubjective reality nor were maliciously disposed toward the great majority of humankind.

> "The difference of natural talents in different men is, in reality, much less than we are aware of; and the very different genius which appears to distinguish men of different professions, when grown up to maturity, is not upon many occasions so much the cause as the effect of the division of labour. The difference between the most

> dissimilar characters, between a philosopher [economist] and a common street porter, for example, seems to arise not so much from nature as from habit, custom, and education. When they came into the world, and for the first six or eight years of their existence, they were perhaps very much alike, and neither their parents nor play-fellows could perceive any remarkable difference. About that age, or soon after, they come to be employed in very different occupations. The difference of talents comes then to be taken notice of, and widens by degrees, till at last the vanity of the philosopher is willing to acknowledge scarce any resemblance" (Smith [1776]1979, Book One, Chapter III, p. 120).

It seems to have gone almost unnoticed that Neoclassical economics turned Smith's principle of division of labour upside down. Instead of the division of labour accounting for differences between individuals, the neoclassicists claim that the differences are already there and account for the kinds of jobs and positions in the work hierarchy that individuals and groups (e.g., races) occupy. The market, so goes their account, tends toward realizing the maximum efficient use of scarce resources, including their optimal development. Of course, it is not claimed that this story holds true in every case, but in the vast majority. This is Neoclassicism's central message: the "free" market system by and large deploys resources, especially human ones, in a manner that best develops and utilizes their capacity to generate output and then pays them the value of their marginal product. According to Neoclassicism, the economic differences between adults are not, as Smith argued, due mainly to the way the market, for whatever reasons, discriminates between similarly endowed individuals, but rather to "the difference of natural talents".

This fundamental disagreement between Smith and the Neoclassicists stems from the even more fundamental one which this chapter has been at pains to illuminate. In offering his principle of the division of labour, Smith assumes, like Du Bois and Beauvoir, that individual identities, and hence the differences between them, are primarily endogenous to the socio-economic process, that is, they are intersubjectively determined. He is not, of course, denying the existence of inherited differences, but rather accepting the fact that the human being is in large part a socio-economic creature, not only in its behaviour but also in its making and remaking. The Neoclassicists, on the other hand, have postulated their axioms in the tradition of high Cartesianism. The economic agent is assumed – and the whole logical superstructure of the Neoclassical enterprise stands on this Cartesian assumption – to enter into economic relations with other economic agents without being changed by them. *Without this assumption, all of Neoclassical economics' additive functions across populations of agents are non-existent.*

Neoclassicism's hypothetical exogenizing of the economic agent resulted in changes in economics infinitely more fundamental than its abandonment of the labour theory of value. Firstly, it effectively walled-off the greater part of the realm of economic phenomena from scholarly and scientific enquiry. In the name of axiomatic certainty, which it mistook for science, economics turned its back on some awkward but central empirical realities. Secondly, this cognitive disaster led to a moral one. Its turning its back on all economics phenomena that are not **intra**subjective, that do not conform to its Cartesian metaphysic, gave rise to a spurious naturalism and the unarticulated but culturally powerful line of racism and sexism that it logically entails (Fullbrook, 2001). As George Akerlof gently puts it, "Neoclassical theory suggests that poverty is the reflection of low initial endowments of human and nonhuman capital" (Akerlof, 2002, p. 412). Poverty, as we all know, is not distributed evenly between races and sexes. So, when it is said that poverty reflects the "low initial endowments" of the people suffering it, a statement is being made about natural differences between races and sexes.

Although the inculcation of such views in the young is morally deplorable, the impetus behind the creation of Neoclassical economics 140 years ago seems to have been entirely innocent. It grew out of the marriage of two exceptionally powerful but rigidly limited strands of thought, the doctrine of the Cartesian or intrasubjective self, with which this chapter has been preoccupied, and the doctrine of Newtonian atomism, whose importance to the Neoclassical project has been widely recognized. But significantly the union of the 17th century's most important metaphysical ideas did not take place for nearly 200 years. By then, the 1870s, the hegemony of both doctrines in their respective fields was waning. The challenge to the

Cartesian self in philosophy and social theory already has been noted. Meanwhile, the development of thermodynamics and Maxwell's magnetic theory meant that the atomistic reductionism of classical mechanics no longer reigned on the frontiers of physics. But not so in the public imagination. Here mechanics was still king, and science was science only to the extent that it mimicked the Newtonian model. William Stanley Jevons [1835-1882], co-founder of Neoclassical economics, was not only drawing on his general training in the natural sciences, but also playing to the public galleries when in the preface to *The Theory of Political Economy* (1871) he wrote:

> "But as all the physical sciences have their basis more or less obviously in the general principles of mechanics, so all branches and divisions of economic science must be pervaded by certain general principles. It is to the investigation of such principles – to the tracing out of *the mechanics of self-interest and utility*, that this essay has been devoted. The establishment of such a theory is a necessary preliminary to any definite drafting of the superstructure of the aggregate science" (emphasis added) (Jevons 1970, p. 50).

Marie Léon Walras [1834-1910] begins and proceeds in the same vain in his *Elements of Pure* Economics (1874-77) Alluding to the role of force and velocity in mechanics, he says:

> Similarly, ... this pure theory of economics is a science which resembles the physico-mathematical sciences in every respect. This assertion is new and will seem strange; but I have just proved it to be true... (Walras 1984, p. 71).

Walras does not have just any mathematics in mind, but rather that of classical mechanics. In applying a mathematics to an empirical domain, the key question for the real scientist is always whether or not the structures described by the former are isomorphic to those found in the latter.

Today the question might never violate the thought processes of an economist trained in *a priorism*. But for Walras, trained as a mining engineer, this question would have been at the forefront of his mind. It is the "proof" of an isomorphism between the differential calculus of classical mechanics and the economic phenomena of the market place (and thus also between economic and mechanical phenomena, i.e., Jevon's "mechanics of self-interest and utility") that Walras sets out to demonstrate at the beginning of his treatise. As he well understood, everything that follows in his book depends on this "proof". Of what does it consist?

Well, of course, nothing empirical. Like Descartes, but in the name of science rather than of philosophy, Walras chooses to proceed definitionally, slicing up the universe into realms and *assigning them* the properties that will yield him his desired "results". We may, he says, "divide the facts of our universe into two categories": "*natural* phenomena" and *"human* phenomena", whose essential difference, he proclaims, is that whereas the former result from "blind and ineluctable forces", the latter result from human will which is "self-conscious and independent" (Walras 1984, p. 61).

By "human will" Walras means the wills of individuals. This is the crucial Cartesian point. It is these wills, as Walras repeats numerous times, which are proclaimed *independent* and thus intrasubjective. But whereas Descartes devised this arrangement to relieve his philosopher's existential angst, Walras needs it to launch economics as "a physico-mathematical science like mechanics" (Walras 1984, p. 71). This Cartesian self is mandatory if economic relations between human personalities are to be imagined as isomorphic to those between Newtonian bodies, that is, interacting but without altering their individual identities. A scientifically legitimate application of the mathematics of classical mechanics to economic phenomena requires this property of atomism. Without it, the individual supply and demand functions are not additive, thereby leaving the market or aggregate supply and demand functions undefined and, indeed, putting market analysis beyond the scope of the theory. But the Neoclassical project's dependence on Cartesianism extends further. It also requires, as Walras emphasizes (pp. 61-2), Descartes' notion of self-consciousness:

> "nothing is more easily or manifestly perceptible to me than my own mind" (Descartes 1970, p. 75).

Post-Freud, no aspect of Cartesianism appears sillier and more untrue than this one. Nonetheless, Neoclassical economics requires the crystalline self-knowledge of the Cartesian self in order to generate its putative functions. Having purged itself of the intersubjective dimension, it has only the self-knowledge of subjects hermetically sealed from influence from other subjects and their institutions to which to appeal for its hypothetical data for its "mechanics of self-interest and utility", for its "physico-mathematical science".

In constructing his "proof", Walras sketched an ontology that guaranteed, as he justly emphasized, the purity of his product. By eliminating the intersubjective, Walras created a make-believe world in which the social dimension of economic agency was decreed from existence. This sociopathic ontology has now dominated economics for over a century. In his back-of-the-envelope style, Walras explicitly defined its basic categories. It divides the entities of the universe "into two great classes: *persons* and *things*. Whoever is not conscious of itself and not master of itself is a thing" (Walras 1984, p. 62). It "divide[s] the facts of our universe into two categories": "*natural* phenomena" and "*human* phenomena" (p. 61). The latter is the product of human wills that are "self-conscious and independent" (p. 61). The "realm of human phenomena" consists of two and only two categories: "human actions in respect to natural forces", e.g., mining, and "relations between persons and persons" (p. 63) whose wills or subjective identities are independent of one another.

As we have seen, in the beginning modern economics did not duck the complexities of economic reality. I do not know when and where its intersubjective tradition began, only that in Adam Smith it was in good heart. And with narrative pluralism the Neoclassical project need not have changed that. Neoclassicism is neither a useless nor an inherently intolerant, anti-scientific undertaking. Pretending that economic agents are radically different from how they are offers one point of view, even if a narrow one, from which to study economic reality. But the pseudo-science and fundamentalism that was already salient in Walras and Jevons became dominant in Neoclassicism and has continued to be so down to the present day. Instead of contributing to a body of knowledge, Neoclassical economics became a mandatory narrative, insisting that in matters economic it offered the only way to the truth. The result has been "a triumph of ideology over science" (Stiglitz 2002b).

In the century since economics' autistic turning many economists have tried, with varying degrees of influence, to effect its rehabilitation. Caroline Foley was the first off the mark. In 1893 she published in *The Economic Journal* a long and elegantly argued article titled "Fashion" (Foley 1893; Fullbrook 1998), which not only called for the re-expansion of economics' conceptual framework so as to include intersubjective demand phenomena, but also pointed out that rising standards of living cause consumer demands to become ever less closely tied to biological needs so that intersubjective factors enter increasingly into demand determination. Late the following year Thorstein Veblen not only took up Foley's challenge but also her approach when he published "The Economic Theory of Woman's Dress", launching in his middle-age the line of intersubjective analysis for which he is celebrated (Veblen 1894). The whole institutionalist school to which Veblen's work gave rise was committed to considering economic agents as social beings. In the United States in the 1920s the Institutionalists briefly threated the Neoclassical hegemony before rapidly losing ground. Keynes's *General Theory* (1936), as well as some more traditional business cycle theories, turned on aggregate intersubjective effects, and with the post-war rise of Keynesianism it appeared that economics might, not just on the margins but in the main, escape from its Cartesian prison. But once again it was not to be. Led by John Hicks and Paul Samuelson, the Neoclassicists marketed an emasculated Keynesian analysis, one without intersubjective agents, and succeeded in turning back the clock. Even John Kenneth Galbraith, whose work added much to the intersubjective tradition, could not reverse or even halt the retrogression. By the end of the 1980s any economist expressing professional concern with the intersubjective dimension of economic reality risked being assigned to the outer reaches of heterogeneity.

But what about the rise of game theory? One might say that because game theory is explicitly about direct interactions between individuals, it is about intersubjectivity. Such reasoning, however, misses the central thrust of this chapter. Classical mechanics is also explicitly about interactions between individuals and how their interactions change their behaviour. The criterion for intersubjectivity methodology is not whether or not interactions take place between human individuals but rather whether those interactions are conceptualized as sometimes changing those individuals' subjective characteristics.

Does game theory conceptualize human agents as intersubjective? In the main, no. It describes how in game-like situations agents choose strategies *given exogenously fixed* utility functions which represent the agents' subjectivities. (This is true even of Lewis, 1969.) But what about "evolutionary" game theory (e.g., Samuelson 2002)? Despite its name, this appears to be a dead-end for intersubjective analysis. A byproduct of evolutionary biology, where the "players" are species and genes, its novel feature is that it treats players as hard-wired with particular strategies and therefore without the freedom to change, not only their ends, but also their strategic means.

A more promising route for bringing game theory to bear on some subset of intersubjective economic phenomena is Thomas Schelling's (1960) "coordination game" approach. André Orléan (2003), seeking to understand "the inter-subjective and self-referential dynamics" (p. 179) of stock markets, has used it to achieve what is in effect a formalization of Keynes's famous beauty contest parable (1936). Drawing on Shiller 1991, Orléan shows how a group belief can emerge autonomously relative to the beliefs of the group's individual members and then become part of those individuals' belief systems.

But there is much more to understanding the role of intersubjectivity in economic reality than formalization, let alone game theory, can reveal. Recent years have witnessed, despite the surge in Neoclassical fundamentalism, new beginnings and growing respectability for intersubjective economics. And the new interest is diverse, not only geographically but also in terms of research programmes and topics: in France the French Intersubjectivists (Aglietta and Orléan 2002; Dupuy 1989, 1991, 2002; Levy 2002; Orléan 1989, 1990, 1992, 1998; Thévenot 2002), in the UK the Critical Realists (Fleetwood 1996; Lawson 1997, 1999; Lewis and

Runde 2002), in the U.S. hybrid offshoots of Critical Realism (Davis 2002), in France, the U.S. and the UK Feminist Economics (Delphy 1984; Delphy and Leonard 1992; Feiner 1994, Nelson 1995; Barker and Feiner 2003); in Switzerland, and elsewhere Experimental Economics (Fehr and Falk 2002; Fehr and Schmidt 1999), in the UK and US a new wave of Institutional Economics (Hodgson 1998, 2002; Mayhew 2002), as well as dispersed and assorted independents (Ackerman 2002; Akerlof 2002; Dow 1990; Fullbrook 2001, 2002, Hargreaves Heap 2002; Kaul 2002; Ormerod 2002; Rizvi 2002; Sofianou 1995; Stiglitz 2002a; Wynarczyk 2002). Will these and other developments lead to freeing economics from Descartes' legacy, enabling it to reconnect with Adam Smith's tradition?

Chapter 3
Concealed ideologies

1. Introduction

There will never be a theory or school of economics that cannot be used ideologically. Ditto for the human and social sciences in general. This susceptibility stems largely from the recursive relations that such disciplines have with their objects of enquiry. These inalienable facts impose upon social scientists, especially those who disseminate their teachings to the young, burdensome ethical responsibilities which in the main have yet to be assumed. This chapter will, by illuminating the structure of the problem, show that only through narrative pluralism can economics curriculums avoid being programmes of ideological indoctrination.

The argument's barebones look like this. As explained in Chapter 1, a knowledge narrative or conceptual system defines, at the exclusion of others, a point of view toward its object of enquiry. For the human sciences this fact poses a moral danger. Their conceptual systems relate to their objects of enquiry in two ways that invite them to play an ideological function as well as an epistemological one. Both of these relations are recursive. First, a social-science conceptual system can alter the objects of its enquiry by becoming part of the conceptual and belief apparatus through which humans define themselves, perceive others and make choices, thereby changing the structures and propensities of the human world. With the spread of mass higher education, this recursive phenomena becomes more common, pervasive and profound. Second, unlike the natural sciences, the human sciences are ultimately a means from on high of preserving or reconstructing the basic realities that they study, these in total being the human project. Different knowledge narratives present different sets of choices, real or imagined, to be chosen and acted upon by human populations at large. It can never be the case that each of these sets of choices will equally favour every group in society. This makes the success of democratic processes dependent on the ethical standards under which the social sciences are dispensed through educational systems.

This chapter's focus on conceptual systems is largely eccentric in the context of the literature on ideology in economics, and its non-traditional conclusions will be uncongenial to a wide spectrum of readers. Traditionally, modern analyses of the connections between economics and ideology emphasize the role played by value judgments of various kinds, be they intentional or not. It is not my purpose here to take issue with that approach. Instead I wish to show that, regardless of value judgments, it is the nature of all social theorizing, economics being no exception, to have ideological content in the sense of favouring some groups in society over others. As explained in Chapter 1, every conceptual framework functions as a limited point of view and because of this social sciences can become the basis of *concealed ideologies*. This chapter will examine how this works, explaining the difference between the ideologically driven fake pluralism found in economics and the real pluralism that created contemporary physics and biology.

2. Degenerate and non-degenerate empiricism

In the social sciences, economics especially, epistemology and ethics are inextricably linked. Within any science, different perspectives on a particular field may suggest different possibilities for human intervention in that field; or they might suggest the same interventions but evaluate them differently. In the social sciences these possibilities relate directly to the human realm and so inevitably pertain to ethical and political judgements. Historically social scientists in general and economists in particular have glossed over this interdependence between their epistemological choices and ramifications for ethical issues.

One can regard economics as a science in a post-Enlightenment sense only to the extent that it is grounded on an empirical epistemology. Empiricism, in the broadest sense, is the idea that experience is fundamental to our knowledge of the world. Unlike rationalism, empiricism exhibits caution regarding claims to knowledge. It refuses notions of privileged access to the world. Instead, it recognizes the eccentricity and incompleteness of all perspectives, and therefore discrepancies between conceptions of things and the things themselves. In lieu of appeals to authority, empiricism democratizes science by making the replication of observations carried out from the same cognitive perspective but by different individuals the criterion of authentic science.

One consequence, often overlooked, of this epistemology is that it relativizes knowledge to the kinds of experiences we have. Experience-based knowledge depends not only on the object of inquiry but also on the *cognitive perspective* (questions asked, criteria for selecting facts, conceptual categories, framework of analysis, etc.) that the inquirer brings to the task. Knowledge arrived at empirically emerges as an entanglement of two sources of inputs, one from the world, be it natural or social, and another from the inquirer.

Human subjectivity does not dissolve when one moves from being a consumer to thinking about and observing the world, not even when thinking about and observing economies. The subjectivity of the human mind is an irreducible feature of reality. Nowhere is this more in evidence than in the practice of empiricism. The problem or question selected for investigation is always someone's problem, whose 'facts' are always a selection from experience, that are then organized into various selected conceptual categories, and which are then subjected to a selected framework of analysis. Inevitably, each of these four selection stages involves value choices influenced by the social context of the selection processes, such as the known predilections of a PhD examining committee, and by the desires and the social, personal and intellectual characteristics of those making the choices.

The significant elements of cognitive perspectives are diverse and open to various combinations, each offering a particular viewpoint on the field of inquiry. By the very nature of scientific practice, scientists utilizing the same cognitive perspective in a field come to see themselves as a group with group interests. If relatively strong in number, such a group may become inclined to promote itself by discouraging or even stopping empirical inquiry in its field from cognitive perspectives, especially promising ones, other than its own. Such a state of affairs constitutes a *degenerate empiricism*, as it wishes to limit inquiry to a single vantage point, thereby holding back the advancement of knowledge.

Degenerate empiricisms are more likely to emerge and persist in the social sciences than in the natural sciences. This tendency exists because, as noted, the possibilities brought to light by the social sciences pertain directly to the human realm and so inevitably suggest or call for the making of ethical and political judgements. Making them would be difficult even if everyone brought the same system of values to bear on the possibilities. But they do not, and so some people will wish to highlight some possibilities and to obscure others. This creates a strong additional source of motivation for restricting empirical inquiry. Individuals both in and out of a science may become ethical or political partisans of the implications suggested by one cognitive perspective and so promote it by blocking the use of others.

Let us explore these ideas in more detail.

In considering cognitive perspectives it helps to highlight the difference between those which are incompatible and those which are merely non-equivalent. Harvard philosopher Hilary Putman explains the difference:

> "But the fact that the contents of a room may be partly described in the terminology of fields and particles and the fact that it may be partly described by saying that there is a chair in front of a desk are not in any way 'incompatible', not even 'at face value': the statements 'the room may be partly described by saying there is a chair in front of a desk' and 'the room may be partly described as consisting of fields and particles' don't even *sound* 'incompatible'. And they are not cognitively equivalent (even if we do not bar the fantastic possibility of defining terms like 'desk' and 'table' in the language of fundamental physics, the field-particle description contains a great deal of information that is not translatable into the language of desks and chairs). That we can use both these schemes without being required to

> reduce one or both of them to some single fundamental and universal ontology is the doctrine of pluralism" (Putnam 2004, pp. 48-9).

3. Roads to ideology

The key adjective in the passage from Putman is "partly". Because any cognitive perspective can only partly describe an object, a non-degenerate empiricism prefers two perspectives to one when they are compatible but not equivalent. Sometimes scientists may prefer to keep two even when they are incompatible, modern physics being the leading example.

The story in economics could not be more different. Historically economists investigating the economics realm from different cognitive perspectives have regarded one another at the very least as rivals and usually as enemies. This is reflected in the custom among economists of referring to pursuits for economic knowledge from different perspectives not as "fields" which complement each other, but as "schools" which do battle against one another. This comes about partly because economists generally are in denial about the partiality of their vision of economic reality, and partly and more importantly because, as noted above, in economics different epistemological choices suggest different ethical/political choices, and the latter are allowed to determine the former.

But we must be careful here. When talking about the social sciences and ideology there is a danger of falling into a logical hole. Because every possible conceptual system can view its social object only from a particular point of view, it is self-defeating to equate ideology with systematized bias *vis-à-vis* the social realm, lest the social sciences are to be regarded as but a subcategory of ideology. As explained in Chapter One, the test of whether or not an economic or social theory is ideological is not its essence nor how and through whom it came to be nor who uses it. Instead the test is *how* it is used.

> "...an approach to economics can be an exercise in ideology or a tool for the advancement of understanding. A

> conceptual system regarding human affairs becomes an ideology when its partisans refuse to countenance the use of other systems as well, as when a group of economists refuse to teach their students how to view the economic realm from conceptual points of view other than the one that they favour."

Ideology consists of this refusal to seriously entertain other conceptual points of view regarding the human world.

It is important to note here how the epistemological and ideological dimensions relate. *An economic theory becomes an ideology precisely at that moment when its partisans decide to curb the growth and prevent the dissemination of knowledge of how to see all those aspects of the economy that their approach leaves in the dark.*

An analysis similar to this seems implicit in the famous French economics students' petition of 2000:

> "Out of all the approaches to economic questions that exist, generally only one is presented to us. This approach is supposed to explain everything by means of a purely axiomatic process, as if this were THE economic truth. We do not accept this dogmatism. We want a pluralism of approaches, adapted to the complexity of the objects and to the uncertainty surrounding most of the big questions in economics (unemployment, inequalities, the place of financial markets, the advantages and disadvantages of free-trade, globalization, economic development, etc.)" (French Students 2000).

This was a call for two things, the realization of each being necessary for the realization of the other: an end to the ideological pretense of there being only one right way of looking at a major part of the human world, and an opening of doors to the knowledge and understanding of the economic realm that comes from taking other narrative perspectives. It is important to note that the students were not asking for the banishment of Neoclassical economics in its epistemological function, only the end of its deployment as an enforced (every student wants a good mark) ideology.

But as Peter Söderbaum explains, ultimately the monopoly of Neoclassical economics undermines democracy:

> "The 'fact' that also ideology is present means that the 'one-paradigm position' at departments of economics becomes untenable. Limiting economics to one paradigm means that one ideological orientation is emphasized at the expense of all others. This position is not compatible with normal ideas of democracy. Departments of economics should avoid the role of being political propaganda centres. With more than one paradigm as part of a pluralistic strategy, the ideological diversity in a democratic society will be better reflected. Furthermore, one specific paradigm, such as the neoclassical one, may perform well in relation to some fields of study while being more of a problem in relation to other fields" (Söderbaum 2004, p. 159)

But these ideological blinkers ultimately also undermine economic performance, and even, as becomes increasingly clear, our survival as a species. The problem is not that Neoclassical economics does not make a substantial contribution to our grasp of economics affairs, but that there is so very much more in the economic realm that needs knowing and understanding. We must take into account not just unchanging atomistic Utilitarian agents acting in a world dominated by equilibrium, but also institutions, intersubjectivity between agents, history, the environment, the ecosystem, geopolitical realities, corporate politics, globalism, strategies of actors and groups, points of view from the South, sociological dimensions including gender and race relations, the heterogeneity of agents, and the importance of economic behaviors based on non-market factors, including power structures, organizations, and cultural and social fields.

There are two ways in which the interdependence between epistemology and ethics in economics may come about. The individual economist may in the first instance already adhere to a particular set of ethical or political beliefs and choose the cognitive perspective (i.e. the school) that lends support to it. Or indoctrination in a particular school may lead the economist to adopt the ethical perspective that it suggests with the result being that he or she comes to disdain attempts to advance economic knowledge from other cognitive perspectives.

4. The tradition of emotive and normative language in Neoclassical economics

Economics' predilection for choosing emotive and normative words, such as "rationality", "choice", "freedom", "equity" and "efficiency", to designate its concepts actively encourages the conflation of epistemological and ethical choices. But it is also the case that the intrinsic interchange between epistemology and ethics in the human sciences makes it extremely difficult at the analytical level *to maintain the distinction between fact and value.* Together these two factors, the one chosen, the other intrinsic, have made it very easy for the Neoclassical narrative to function as an ideology.

For example, Neoclassical economics, especially in its more formalistic forms, is founded on the strictly normative idea that an optimum or preferred state is always a maximum or a minimum. Seldom is it presented in the classroom as such. But this omission may be due to ignorance more often than to ethical failure. Genuine confusion here emerges easily because of the collective unawareness of the fact that in the social sciences epistemological choices suggest ethical ones. A look at the maximum/minimum analytical framework illustrates the point.

With the advent of Samuelson's tautological concept of revealed preferences, Neoclassical economics tried to unhook itself from utilitarianism so as to champion itself as value-free. Even if our age is less credulous of such claims, it remains easy to miss the primary source of the implicit value structure. Although many Neoclassicalists dispensed with the cardinal utility concept, their analysis remained wedded to the same notion of optimum (and equilibrium and methodological individualism) *because that was the only one their maxima/minima calculus, borrowed from classical mechanics, permitted.* In the context of physical bodies, that calculus is ethically neutral, but when applied to human affairs and when the value-laden word "optimum" is attached to those maxima and minima, the calculus becomes ethically charged.

Even so, this need not create a problem. One can dream of the day when economists, like physicists, refuse to indulge degenerate empiricism. If other (non-Neoclassical) narrative frameworks were presented and some of the possibilities that they outlined were acknowledged as alternatives to the Neoclassical "optimums", so that facts (e.g. maximums) were distinguished from preferred states (e.g. Neoclassical optimums), then the conflation between fact and value, now endemic, would be much less likely to result. This example illustrates the general case: without pluralism it is impossible for economics to maintain the distinction between fact and value.

Of course the conflation of fact and value that takes place under degenerate empiricism in the social sciences is not always inadvertent. Sometimes, when the ethos permits, it results from a more deliberate use of language and so raises ethical questions on a more personal but nonetheless epistemological level. But whether accidental or deliberate, merging the ethical and epistemological dimensions of a body of knowledge generated by a degenerate empiricism is the standard recipe for making an ideology. In economics any cognitive perspective could be used to this end and many have, some notoriously, like Marxist economics in the past and Neoclassical economics today. Because of the latter's current stranglehold on the economics profession, it makes sense to turn to it for examples of degenerate practice. I will consider four.

Rational choice

The Newtonian metaphysics of Neoclassical economics if known would embarrass many partisans of liberal democracy. Like Newton's, the Neoclassical model presumes determinacy. This requires that the properties of its determinants be fixed. In both theories the determinants are individuals, in Newton's case bodies and in Neoclassical economics persons. Obviously this condition is inconsistent with freedom of choice. This does not necessarily obviate the usefulness of this cognitive approach in economics if practiced non-degenerately. But when the approach mutates into an ideology, this attribute becomes a serious liability and so requires concealment.

For this concealment, Neoclassical economics has invented an elaborate rhetorical device. Conjoining two emotive words, it coined the term "*rational choice*" to refer to a situation in which its model precludes the possibility of choice. "Rationality" means that an agent's "choices" are in conformity with an ordering or scale of preferences. The 'rational' agent is required to "choose" among the alternatives available that option which is highest-ranking. "Rational behaviour" here means behaviour in accordance with some prior ordering of alternatives in terms of relative desirability.

For this approach to have any predictive power, it must be assumed that the preferences do not change during the period of time being considered. So the basic condition of Neoclassical rationality is that individuals must *forego* choice in favour of some past reckoning, thereafter acting as automata.

This conceptual elimination of freedom of choice, in both its everyday and philosophical meanings, gives Neoclassical theory the hypothetical determinacy that its Newtonian inspired metaphysics require. No indeterminacy; no choice. No determinacy; no Neoclassical model. The Neoclassical contrivance of "rational choice" is an example, an extreme one admittedly, of what can happen when in the social sciences a cognitive perspective becomes degenerate.

Efficiency

Like rationality, nearly everyone considers "*efficiency*" a good idea. It is hard to imagine a more value-laden word. This makes the word attractive to many economists, especially when addressing the public. Yet the meaning of "efficiency" always depends on what one chooses to count. Members of the public are inclined to believe that economists use the word to mean approximately what they themselves construe. This is seldom the case. For example, suppose five firms all manage to lower by the same amounts the production cost and selling price of a standard product that they all produce. One does it by cutting its workers' pay, another by working employees longer hours, another by getting materials at lower prices from a poorer country, another by replacing some of its workers with robots and another by inventing machinery improvements that allow it to cut work hours with no loss of output, profit, jobs or pay. Are all of these changes equally efficient (or inefficient)? A Neoclassical economist would answer yes, because the five firms all end up producing the same product at the same cost and selling it at the same price. For them that is all that matters.

Market

In Neoclassical economics the term "*market*" is habitually used, sometimes in the same sentence, often in the same paragraph, to signify both a brute fact (as in "the Chinese market for mobile phones") and a normative and hence ethical idea as when a government is said to interfere with "the market's free operation" or "the market is distorted and its prices artificial". This rhetorical bridging of the is/ought divide is a powerful device, be it intentional or not, for ideological indoctrination. Do economists, especially those who teach, have an ethical obligation to avoid encouraging such conflations between facts and their ethical values?

Economic growth

Like the term "market", the Neoclassical mainstream uses the term "*economic growth*" in both a factual and a normative sense, so the one meaning has come to infer the other. It presumes that "economic growth" always represents a good thing. The mainstream defines the term precisely, it being any increase in a country's gross or net national product. Yet the implications of this definition are seldom apparent as a few examples illustrate.

If families decide to forgo home-cooked meals in favour of more expensive fast-food ones, their additional expenditure counts as economic growth. If parents decide to pay for a nursery to care for their children instead of continuing to do so themselves, the amount they pay for the care counts as economic growth. Even more worrying, social breakdown, epidemics and pollution are treated as engines of economic growth. Social breakdown leads to increased expenditures for prisons, police and alarm systems. Epidemics result in increased expenditure for medicines and stays in hospitals. Pollution and congestion lead to huge expenditures to escape them, for example, commuting from the suburbs, double glazing and air-conditioning. All of these phenomena, which most ethical systems would deplore, contribute significantly to economic growth as defined by the Neoclassical mainstream, which holds it to be a good thing.

Expenditure incurred in repairing environmental damage caused by human activity is often called "defensive expenditure". Jean Gadrey explains how the ecological economist, beginning from a different epistemological position, casts these expenditures in another ethical light, from an ecological perspective:

> "[E]xpenditure (and the corresponding output) incurred in repairing the damage caused by human actions should not be counted as a positive contribution to 'real' wealth. If such damage (pollution, crime, road accidents, etc.) reduces well-being and makes it necessary to produce goods and services (whose value is X) in order to repair or defend, there can be no question of X being counted as a positive item in any measurement of 'real' wealth. And since the conventional measure of GDP counts the defensive output X as a positive item, which is acceptable from a purely economic perspective, X must be deducted from GDP in order better to identify 'real' wealth (that which contributes to well-being)" (Gadrey 2004, pp. 265-6).

Of course the suggestion here is not that Neoclassical economists favour social breakdown, epidemics, pollution and ecological collapse. Rather, these are illustrations of how in the social sciences cognitive perspectives, quite innocent in and of themselves, can lead, intended or otherwise, to ethical positions. Each of the four examples has an epistemological dimension and an ethical one. But when the knowledge base from which the ethical discussions take place is tightly controlled, the outcomes of those discussions are in effect prearranged. This is a standard tactic of ideologies in general and of Neoclassical economics in particular. By refusing to recognize the legitimacy of economic knowledge coming from narrative perspectives other than its own, Neoclassical economics forces ethical questions into a framework of controlled ignorance and thereby predetermines their "answers".

5. Concluding remarks

In economics, no less than in other fields, empiricism offers the possibility of making different epistemological choices when approaching an object of inquiry. Because each approach views the economic realm from a different perspective (areas of interest, procedures of observation, categories of facts and analytical frameworks) they create different representations of the economy, all of them partial, some or all of them useful and each egregiously inaccurate if it categorically denies the legitimacy of other representations. This by itself would be bad enough. But in economics, as in other social sciences, degenerate empiricism subverts and in many cases pre-empts ethical debate by concealing possible configurations of and actions in the human realm and also by generally obfuscating the distinction between fact and value. In these ways, what should be a pursuit of knowledge is subverted into the construction and dissemination of ideology.

Economists of all varieties must, like physicists and biologists have done, learn to live without the belief that there is one right way of describing and explaining reality. Natural scientists have found it worthwhile to accept this existential burden for purely epistemological reasons. For economists there is, if they are genuinely of a democratic persuasion, an additional reason because economics as a discipline impacts on the object of its enquiry. Because each narrative looks at the economic from a particular conceptual angle, different narratives will, *when presented to the public as* ***the*** *truth*, promote the interests of different groups in society over others, encourage and discourage in individuals different types of behaviour, illuminate or leave in the dark different problems and possibilities for humankind, and etc. In other words, when economic theories are handled in this way they function primarily not as part of a set of tools for human enlightenment, but, to the contrary, as *concealed ideologies*, which, when one wins out over the rest, smother real discussion, silence debate, blind the public to most of economic reality, and ultimately place the human project at risk.

Chapter 4

From the natural to the social

> "in human society nothing is natural" (Simone de Beauvoir 1989, p. 725).

1. Introduction

In this chapter I am going to consider two usages of the word "naturalism" in the social sciences, and the relation of these usages to conceptual issues in economics. In the current Anglo-American usage of the word "naturalism", I am a naturalist. But in the continental usage I am an anti-naturalist.[1] This contradiction exists because philosophical naturalism has two strands of argument that social scientists usually deploy separately. Firstly, in the social sciences there is *epistemological naturalism*. It originates with Auguste Comte in the first half of the 19th century, and argues for using the procedures and the methods of explanation of the natural sciences in other fields of study. For example, Tony Lawson argues for a non-dogmatic variety of epistemological naturalism in his book *Economics and Reality* (1997). He holds that "the study of social objects can be scientific in the sense of natural science," but that there may be "significant differences in methods appropriate to studying social and natural objects" (Lawson 1997, p. 60) I am a "naturalist" in this Lawsonian sense.

However, Lawson's phrase, "social and natural objects", brings us to the second usage of the term "naturalism". Traditionally, philosophical naturalism, whose origins are pre-Socratic, justifies its epistemological dimension on ontological or metaphysical grounds. It argues that nature should be viewed as an all-inclusive sphere without incursions from outside

[1] The work of the French social theorist, Christine Delphy, epitomizes current Continental usage of "naturalism" and anti-naturalist analysis. It also has had a formative influence on this essay. For recent examples of the Continental usage and for critiques of "naturalist explanation" in the social sciences see Delphy's *Close to Home*, 1984; Chaperon, 1997; Kail, 2001; and Armengaud, 2001.

and that methods of inquiry should reflect this ontological monism. Thus, in the 17th century when the naturalist tradition re-emerged, it first had to reject the notion of divine will. Triumphant, it next took on human will. Human beings were to be viewed exclusively through naturalist psychologies, like those of Locke, Hobbs and Hume, and all social phenomena were to be regarded as *a subclass of the natural order.* I call this doctrine ontological naturalism. It is what most contemporary continental social theorists mean by "naturalism", and by which I could be classed an "anti-naturalist". So too could anyone who, like Lawson, feels comfortable with his phrase "social *and* natural objects". According to the tenets of *ontological naturalism*, this phrase, like "oranges and fruit", is a type of category mistake.

Very briefly, I am going to do three things with this distinction between two kinds of naturalism. First, I am going to sketch the history of contemporary ontological anti-naturalism, or at least the branch of it with which I am familiar. Second, I am going to identify and consider the significance of four naturalist concepts in economics: biological notions of race and gender difference, determinism and atomism. Third, I am going to make the dual case that when carried to its logical conclusion, epistemological naturalism implies **ontological anti-naturalism** and that, without it, economics is largely incapable of addressing contemporary human issues.

2. History of ontological anti-naturalism

The origins of contemporary ontological ant-naturalism are diverse and open to dispute. Certainly they include the prolonged intellectual dissent that culminated in the French Revolution. And in Great Britain there were the 18th-century radical liberals who created the successful anti-slavery movement. The ideas of these Europeans and their influence on America have been much written about.

Less well-known, but more relevant to understanding recent anti-naturalist social thought, is the tradition that emerged in mid-19th-century America among African-American intellectuals that I drew upon in the previous chapter. Against the notion of race as a biological concept, black abolitionists developed a concept of race as a social construct. This says that, in the main, observable differences between the races are socially and economically constructed rather than natural or innate. Already in the 1840s for example, the concept of socially constructed racial difference structures the writing of Frederick Douglass (Douglass, 1997). By the end of the 19th century this anti-naturalism was a standard ingredient of African-American social thought,[2] and at the beginning of the 20th century W. E. B. Du Bois gave this tradition's socio-economic concept of race an academic presence.[3] Nevertheless, the conceptual displacement from the natural to the social failed to affect white mainstream social theory. Both in America and in Europe, "racial" differences continued to be treated as natural givens, rather than part of the domain of socio-economic phenomena to be explained. There was, writes Henry Louis Gates, "the shared assumption among intellectuals that 'race' was a 'thing,' an ineffaceable quantity, which irresistibly determined the shape and contour of thought and feelings as surely as it did the shape and contour of human anatomy" (Gates, 1992, pp. 46-7).

But African-American thinkers persisted with their social concept of race, and in the 1940s this led to two events that decisively changed the intellectual landscape. First, was the massive study of American race relations, *An American Dilemma*, compiled under the direction the Swedish economist Gunnar Myrdal. Myrdal's team included a number of African-Americans, who succeeded in introducing their race concept into the landmark work. Furthermore, Myrdal, referring to the question of racial difference and to the African-American tradition of social thought, wrote that "modern research has tended to confirm the Negroes' view and not the whites'" (Myrdal et. al. 1944, pp. 95-6). Publication of *An American Dilemma* meant that for the first time the African-American anti-naturalist approach to

---

[2] Other relevant African-American writers of this period include Martin Robinson Delany (*The Condition, Elevation, Emigration and Destiny of the Colored people of The United States*) and Alexander Crummell (1819-1898) who, born New York City and the grandson of a west African king, graduated from Queen's College, Cambridge in 1853. Like Douglass, Delany also worked for women's rights; 500,000 copies of his essay "The Black Woman of the South: Her Neglects and Needs" were printed.

[3] Du Bois was a prolific writer for whom there now exists a large secondary literature. I recommend Bell, Grosholz and Stewart, 1996.

race broke through the color-line and entered into white intellectual discourse.

The second decisive event connects with the first. In 1946 Richard Wright, the African-American novelist and essayist, visited France as a guest of the French government. There he became good friends with Simone de Beauvoir, who visited him in New York the following year. Wright showed her around the city, and while doing so, gave her a crash course in African-American social theory. She was 39 and thinking of writing an essay on women. For several years she had been working without great success to expand her theory of intersubjectivity into one with a broad social dimension. But now, sitting at a table at the Savoy dance hall on Harlem's Lenox Avenue, she listened to Wright expound a social-constructionalist explanation of race and race relations that fitted perfectly with her own smaller scale anti-essentialist analysis. Wright also gave her a list of books to read. One was Myrdal's *An American Dilemma*.[4]

Beauvoir quickly generalized this African-American theory of race into the general concept of the Social Other, which she sets out in the Introduction to *The Second Sex* (1949).

---

[4] Sylvia Beach, owner of the famous English language Paris bookshop and lending library, Shakespeare and Company, introduced Beauvoir to Wright's work in 1940. Wright's masterpiece, *Native Son*, published March 1940, arrived in the last shipment of books before the beginning of the Nazi Occupation in June. In 1946, Beauvoir, prior to her American travels, edited a special issue of her journal *Les Temps Modernes* featuring articles and extracts by African-American writers. Following Wright's tutelage in New York, Beauvoir toured the States coast-to-coast by Greyhound Bus, along the way lecturing on philosophy at a score of colleges and universities. But Beauvoir's primary purpose was to observe America, especially its women and its race relations. The latter she increasingly viewed through the conceptual framework gained from Richard Wright.
Returning to Paris, Beauvoir wrote, in three months, *America Day by Day* (1948), a 500-page account of her travels. Here she relates her formative discussions with Wright and details their influence on her observations of social patterns in America, especially in the South. This book was translated and published in full in the United Kingdom in 1952. The following year the same translation was published in the United States, but, under the influence of McCarthyism, was heavily expurgated. Beauvoir's account of her assimilation, through Wright, of African-American social theory, and her theory-laden descriptions of race relations were cut. In effect, part of the book's intellectual heart of was ripped out. A new and unexpurgated English translation was published in 1998 by the University of California (Simons 1999; Tidd 1999; Beauvoir 1968, 1998; Fullbrook and Fullbrook 2000; 2001).

> "Otherness is a fundamental category of human thought [such that] no group ever sets itself up as the One without at once setting up the Other over against itself" (xxiii).

She identifies this relation as the process by which groups of people are "defined and differentiated," (xxiii) and then applies this anti-naturalist or social-constructionalist approach to the question: "what is a woman?" (xxi).

These two anti-naturalist developments, the discrediting of the naturalist views of race and gender, opened up and illuminated with theoretical self-consciousness, huge expanses of social phenomena which previously had been largely closed and invisible to the social sciences. The narratives based on naturalist concepts which had obscured these domains had prevented their rational study just as effectively as once dominant theological narratives had blocked inquiry into the workings of the physical universe.

A word of caution is needed here. Ontological anti-naturalism does not deny the significance of biological differences. For example, *The Second Sex* emphasizes the relevance of biological differences to the historical development and redevelopment of genders. Instead, what ontological anti-naturalists *deny* is that the meanings given to biological features and the choices made for responding to them are biologically determined. It is here, in possibilities for human choice, that they locate the social origin of social phenomena.

3. Naturalist concepts in economics

a. Race and gender

Economics, however, has not yet liberated itself from ontological naturalism. The Neoclassical narrative, which remains hegemonic, is infected to its core with naturalist concepts. These include the naturalist concepts of race and gender. This hardly counts as surprising, given that the Neoclassical narrative was invented before the spread of the conceptual revolutions that I have just described. Naturalist concepts of race and gender function in

Neoclassical theory as tacit but, nonetheless, fundamental assumptions. The way they do so is not immediately obvious.

Traditionally, economics defines itself as the study of the problem of using scarce resources as efficiently as possible so as to maximize output. Its notion of efficient resource allocation emphasizes the optimal development of resources, the optimal division and specialization of labour, and the system of reward. People, the story goes, over the long run realize through education and training their potential as instruments of production. The economic system deploys these human resources in a manner that best utilizes their capacity to generate output, and then, by and large, pays them the value of their marginal product. Of course, no one claims that this theory holds true in every case or in all its details. But it is presented as explaining most of the economic facts most of the time, and as being the state of affairs to which a free market economy approaches.

But if this theory is true, then other less wholesome propositions necessarily follow. Historically, western market economies have been characterized by gendered and racial divisions and hierarchies of labour. Market economies have treated different gender and racial groups very dissimilarly with respect to educational opportunities, their place in the labour market, their opportunities for advancement, their treatment in their place of work, their position in chains of command, and most especially in their rates of reward. These points are not contentious. These race and gender based divisions of labour and the resulting economic differences between white males and the others have been documented by thousands of statistical studies. Nor are we talking about marginal exceptions, but instead about the general case. For example, in the United States the economy has found nearly two-thirds of the adult population wanting *vis-à-vis* white males. The implications for Neoclassicalism are clear. If, over the long run, market economies necessarily allocate resources in the efficient manner claimed, then the observed economic differences between races and between the sexes is due to natural differences. In this way, Neoclassical economics is founded on and dependent upon naturalist concepts of race and gender.

With rare exceptions, people entering university in the 1950s and early 1960s were not uncomfortable with these hard-core racist and sexist propositions. The broad and innate inferiority of women to men was one of those things, like the Sun orbiting the Earth, that had been part of a common-sense understanding of the world for millennia. Nor even in the North of the United States was the received wisdom regarding people of color less dismissive. Nor was one ever for long allowed to forget these verities, because at every level they were realized, enforced and passed on in socio-economic structures. The idea that the observed economic hierarchies between races and between genders was a creation of the socio-economic system, rather than a manifestation of natural differences was for most people, even without McCarthyism, unthinkable.

These days, Neoclassicalists like to talk about racial and sexual discrimination as if they were private matters of spontaneous individual taste, things that originate outside the economic system, rather than propensities created and perpetuated by it.[5] Cynically, this ignores the historical facts. The slave trade, founded on the notion of "human capital", was a vast market operation led by businessmen across western Europe. In the United States, as elsewhere, racial oppression and discrimination has always been for mostly about economics. The racial stratification of America was created by its *economic* institution of slavery, which thrived for over 300 years as part of a free and unregulated market economy. It was conceived, developed and maintained by agrarian entrepreneurs as a means of maximizing their profits and accumulating capital. It worked according to the principles of market exchange, the exchange of slaves. And although ended by government market intervention, the legacy of those centuries of economic practice lives on in contemporary institutions.

Likewise with gender. Economic institutions are primary vehicles for definition and transmission of gender. They, not biology or spontaneous individualist bigotry, determine whether women are or are not allowed to be employed outside the home, and, if they are, what training and what kinds of jobs are open to them, what their rates of pay are, and what kinds of images they are allowed to assume and project.

---

[5] For a well-formed post-Neoclassical approach to the economics of gender, see Delphy and Leonard 1992, especially chapters 4, 5 and 6.

Epistemologically, the point that matters with these two naturalist concepts is a simple one. When racial and gender stratification in the economic sphere are taken as natural givens, as Neoclassical economics tacitly does, then huge classes of economic phenomena disappear from economics' view. It is only by displacing these naturalist concepts with socio-economic ones, that these phenomenal realms become accessible to human understanding.

b. Determinacy

Determinacy is a third naturalist concept structuring mainstream Neoclassical economics. Unlike race and gender, this one is out in the open. Neoclassical economists make no secret of their commitment to pursuing economic knowledge under the presumption of determinate solutions. As explained in Chapter One, the ancestry of this determinist metaphysic, the insistence that the world be regarded as a determinant chain of events, includes both traditional African cultures and Aristotle's *Poetics*. The determinism embodied in many scientific theories is simply a variation of this sensibility regarding narrative and the connection of events. Since the 1870s, economics has appealed to these scientific usages, especially classical mechanics, to justify its insistence upon theories and analysis built on the determinist concept and to give it a naturalist pedigree. To non-economists, this has always seemed a curious position to take regarding human choice and action. It also, as explained in Chapter 1, presumes an ignorance of modern science, which, in fact, drops the concept of determinism when confronted with phenomena that the concept does not fit. Some happenings in the natural world, natural scientists have found, are not always describable and understandable as emanating from a predetermined chain of events. Observation may repeatedly reveal gaps in such chains or chance convergences of two or more chains, showing elements of unpredictability or randomness in reality. Not only micro physics, but also evolutionary theory from Darwin onwards relies heavily on the use of the concept of indeterminism.[6]

It is important to appreciate why the natural sciences have displaced the determinist concept in these areas. It is not for ideological or philosophical

---

[6] See Runde 1999 for a fascinating account of the evolution of Popper's thought regarding the determinism/indeterminism question.

reasons. Rather it is because without this conceptual displacement wide realms of natural phenomena would have remained unknowable. In the natural sciences the desire for this knowledge and for the advantages it would bring to humankind triumphed over narrative fixation. In economics, where the proportion of indeterminate phenomena is much greater, a similar desire and goodwill has not prevailed.

c. Human beings as atoms

A forth strategic naturalist concept in economics is its notion of atomized agents. Much has been written about the Newtonian origins of the Neoclassical *homo economicus* (Hodgson 1993; Fullbrook 1997; 1998a, 1998b; Lawson 1997). No concept in the social sciences is more conspicuously naturalist than this one. The notion of the economic agent as, in Veblen's words, "an isolated definitive human datum" was developed on the basis of an analogy with Newton's conception of materiality. In classical mechanics material bodies interact, but only in the very limited way permitted by the doctrine of atomism. This is the idea that the world is made up of entities whose qualities are completely independent of their relations with other entities. The entities of classical mechanics have mechanical relations and no more. The naturalist concept of atomism, when applied to the socio-economic realm, defines a world in which there are no intersubjective relations, that is, where the subjective properties of the individual agents, such as their tastes and desires, are formed and maintained always independently of the behavior of others, and of institutions and of the market process. Obviously, this is a narrative world which, when applied to advanced market economies, blocks from view a large proportion of economic phenomenon.

4. Conclusion: epistemological naturalism implies ontological anti-naturalism

Taken together, these four naturalist concepts – atomism, determinism, and biologically determined race and gender differences have created an economics that turns its back on most economic phenomena. By contrast, the history of the natural sciences is one of discovering classes of phenomena that do not fit existing concepts and require new narratives. Rather than declaring such phenomena non-natural, so as to excuse self-confinement to the conceptual frameworks favoured by previous generations, natural scientists invent new narrative concepts that bring additional spheres of the natural world – even if only partially – into the realm of the known and the understood. This narrative pluralism has for a century and a half been fundamental to the epistemology of the natural sciences.

There is a great difference between regarding narrative concepts as totems to which one owes allegiance, and regarding them as tools for gaining knowledge. If regarded as tools, then old narratives that ill-fit empirical realms of new interest can be displaced by narratives created and chosen especially for their suitability to the objects of inquiry. Conceptual autonomy, meaning that concepts are invented, crafted and chosen to fit the class of phenomena being studied, has long been epistemologically dominant in and between the natural sciences. Not so in economics, where key concepts are mere hand-me-downs from the distant early days of the natural sciences, and which are as ill-serving to the advancement of economic knowledge as were theological concepts to physics. Only by purging itself of ontological naturalism can economics confront most economic phenomena; only by confronting economic phenomena can economics speak to contemporary human issues. Without conversion to epistemological naturalism and thereby to social economics, most of economic reality remains beyond economics' analytical range. This returns us to where this chapter began. I am *an ontological anti-naturalist* because only by being one can I legitimately claim to be, on the one hand, an epistemological naturalist and, on the other, an economist broadly concerned with contemporary economics issues.

Chapter 5

Narrative rationality

> "The propositions of economic theory ... are obviously deductions from a series of postulates. ... The main postulate of the theory of value is the fact that individuals can arrange their preferences in an order, and in fact do so. These are not postulates the existence of whose counterpart in reality admits of extensive dispute once their nature is fully realised" (Lionel Robbins 1935).

> "I know that the laws of the mind are the same for all men. But it does not seem to me that there is only one way of judging sanely; that depends on the postulates that each has admitted either explicitly or implicitly; and the choice of these postulates is left to each one; it depends on his temperament, on his sensitivity, on this irreducible given that constitutes the individuality of each one" (Simone de Beauvoir 2006, diary entry for 10 July 1927, aged 19).

1. Introduction

Every conceptual scheme or metaphysic, whatever the domain of knowledge, has a limited range of useful application. Only the very foolish would argue that Neoclassical rationality is an exception. Major scientific advances have always been tied, on the one hand, to realizations that a particular conceptual framework was inadequate or incomplete visa-visa some range of empirical phenomena, and, on the other, to the intellectual courage and integrity of men and women to take up the challenges which such realizations present. This chapter, rather than attacking the logical validity of Neoclassical rationality, seeks to reveal its acute and ever increasing limitations. It is hoped that this will encourage the development and use of other conceptual frameworks enabling a greater range of economic choice behaviour to be brought under systematic study *and* included in theories of market outcomes.

The inspiration for the reflections behind this long chapter came mainly from four articles: Foley 1893, Morgenstern 1948, Sofianou 1995, and S. Dow 1995. As a group these works do not form part of any recognized tradition. But it seems epistemologically noteworthy, because statistically it is so improbable, that three out of these four economists are women.

This chapter considers the practice of defining "economic rationality" so as to rationalize a given narrative's belief in some "ideal" state of affairs. Various schools of economics share this approach to "rationality". Five such applications – the Physiocratic, the Marxist, most especially the Neoclassical, the Post SMD Neoclassical and Game Theory – are considered in separate sections. These are followed by the identification of a general paradox, with serious ethical implications, found in narrative approaches to rationality. Next comes a brief section noting how the present critique of rationality differs from earlier ones. This is followed by the chapter's longest section, an explication of eight categories of decision making behaviour judged irrational by the Neoclassical definition, but not by the general populace. The chapter concludes by arguing that common-sense, situational conceptions of rationality have greater explanatory power.

2. Physiocratic rationality

The 18th-century Physiocrats claimed they had discovered principles for organizing a society and its economy in the manner "obviously most advantageous to mankind" (Quesnay [1765]1949, p. 100). This confidence, so widely emulated by economists ever since, mushroomed from an exotic compost of Cartesian rationalism and Augustinian Neoplatonism. The Supreme Being, argued Françoise Quesnay and others, has created in this world an ideal universe which we can turn to our ultimate advantage if through reason we become cognizant of its "unchangeable and unbreakable" laws (Quesnay 1949, p. 100). This knowledge included recognition of the desirability of the following: promotion of agricultural investment, encouragement of exports of and higher prices for agricultural products, deterrence of wages rising above subsistence level, discouragement of investment in commerce and manufacturing, condemnation of unnecessary consumption, preservation of traditional systems of land ownership, maintenance of despotic government, and recognition of the fact that agriculture is the only source of wealth. For the Physiocrats, reasoned application of this knowledge *is economic rationality*. Further, each man's liberty is proportional to his command of this rationality. Thus Quesnay writes:

> "It is therefore obvious that *the natural right* of each man *extends in proportion to his observance of the best laws possible, which constitute the order most beneficial to men in society*. ... Man cannot reasonably refuse the obedience he owes to these laws; otherwise his liberty would be only a liberty detrimental to himself and to others; it would be no more than the liberty of a madman ..." (Quesnay 1949, p. 102).

What stands out as significant here is not the Physiocrats' particular notion of rationality, but rather that *they derive it from their belief in their confident identification of an "essential order"*. For example, few people living either today or in 18th-century France would perceive encouraging the manufacture of desired goods or the raising of wages above subsistence level as manifestly irrational behaviour. Instead, assent to such judgements only comes through faith that such apparently rational behaviour interferes with some larger and preferred order of reality revealed by a holistic vision. Rather than forming its notion of economic rationality after examining and generalizing from the consequences of individual acts, Physiocracy regarded human acts as rational or irrational according to their compatibility with a particular conception of economic reality as a whole.

3. Marxist rationality

Whereas Physiocratic wisdom saw itself as stripping away human illusion to reveal the path to the best of all possible stationary states, Marx, a century later, argued that no amount of human knowledge and contrivance can arrest the teleological laws which inexorably determine a dynamic economic history. As a creature of the capitalist era, his account focused on the destiny of the capitalist system. Its *telos* is breakdown and disintegration, and knowing this is the key to rational behaviour. Under the Marxist view, rational behaviour is dependent on understanding the nature and laws of economic destiny, that is, historical materialism. Understanding it and knowing about the inevitable events to which it leads enables individuals to act and plan their lives in accordance with historical forces. "Those men alone," explains Isaiah Berlin in his account of Marxist thought, "are rational who identify themselves with the progressive, i.e. ascendant class in their society, either, if need be, by deliberately abandoning their past and allying themselves with it, or, if history has already placed them there, by consciously recognising their situation and acting in the light of it" (Berlin 1978, p. 6).

Although, for Marxists, in the long run there is no stopping historical laws, their operation may be hampered or hastened by human acts. Marx explained this as follows:

> "At a certain stage of their development, the material productive forces of society come into conflict with the existing relations of production ... At that point an era of social revolution begins. With the change in the economic foundation the whole immense superstructure is more slowly or more rapidly transformed" (Marx 1976, pp. 3-4).

"[M]ore slowly or more rapidly", that is the narrow stage of indeterminacy on which human volition, irrational and rational, plays its part in history. Quite simply, rational behaviour is behaviour which oils history's inherent tendencies.

Like the Physiocratic notion of rationality, the Marxist variety leads to judgements ill-fitting with individual lives. For example, Marx's attitude toward efforts to raise wages was only marginally less antithetical than Quesnay's. "The general tendency of capitalist production," says Marx, "is not to raise, but sink the average standard of wages" (Marx 1975, p. 78). Marxism regards this "tendency", to drive down wages to an intolerable level, as a primary force bringing about capitalism's collapse and the next and final stage in human history. Consequently, Marx described the trade union rallying call "A fair day's wage for a fair day's work!" as a "*conservative* motto" (Marx 1975, p. 78). Raising wages might slow the process of revolution. Therefore, to do or advocate such a thing was irrational.

4. Neoclassical rationality[1]

No less than Physiocrats and Marxists, Neoclassicalists emphasize presumed inherent tendencies of economic systems as wholes. Inspired by Newtonian mechanics, they conceive of economic systems, ranging from individual markets to whole economies, as self-regulating relationships whose constituent elements tend toward equilibrium. Kenneth Arrow identifies two:

> "aspects of the notion of general equilibrium as it has been used in economics: (1) the simple notion of determinateness ... and (2) the more specific notion that each relation represents a balance of forces" and "that a violation of any one relation sets in motion forces tending to restore the balance" (Arrow 1983b, p. 107).

As Arrow's description indicates, equilibrium in Neoclassical economics serves as much more than just a concept; it is also a sweeping hypothesis about the nature of economic reality, especially about the operation of whole systems. We need to look closer at what this entails for "rationality".

Neoclassicalism begins *a priori* with a conception of markets and economies, including all relationships between their various component magnitudes, *as determinate systems ruled by a principle of equilibrium*. This holistic metaphysic, which I will call the *Equilibrium Hypothesis*, imposes

---

[1] In addition to the usual axioms of independence, transitivity and completeness of preferences, this chapter includes under this heading Simon's concept of "bounded rationality", because it has been developed largely as a special case of Neoclassical rationality. But this does not preclude its application to other narrative concepts of rationality, nor, indeed, to that of non-narrative rationality as developed in this chapter's final section (Simon 1955; 1976).

tight logical requirements on the definition of the elements of a system and on the relationships between their magnitudes. These impositions of the macro vision on micro elements are especially strict when it comes to the application of mathematical procedures to the construction of models. Hence, one finds embedded in general equilibrium models a long list of stipulations regarding the micro elements, including pure competition, constant coefficients of production, identical products and methods of production within an industry, perfect markets or instantaneous omniscience, perfect divisibility of goods, and, of course, perfect "rationality" for economic agents. Some combination of these and other micro conditions must be true before the Equilibrium Hypothesis conceivably can be true. In other words, the "heroic" micro assumptions contribute to making logically possible the set of equilibrium prices and quantities predetermined by the narrative's holistic and *a priori* starting point.

The Equilibrium Hypothesis requires a further hypothesis postulating some driving force behind the putative order. Neoclassicalism, rather than appealing to a Supreme Being like the Physiocrats or to historical materialism like Marxists, asserts that the determining force is the independently "chosen" behaviour of individual economic agents. I will call this the *Individual Behaviour Hypothesis*. For Neolassicalists it is agents acting individually which results in determinate equilibrium values for markets. But, as noted above, this outcome is logically possible only if the behaviour of individual agents is circumscribed by various formal properties. Therefore, "deriving" these properties, with minimum metaphysical fuss and with emphasis on the behaviour of consumers, has always stood at the center of the Neoclassical project. And it is precisely these properties and the class of behaviour which they define that the Neoclassical narrative tendentiously calls "rationality" and "rational economic behaviour". Likewise, behaviour inconsistent with the Equilibrium Hypothesis is dubbed "irrational". Having found out what kind of individual behaviour could make the Equilibrium Hypothesis true and having limited "rational behaviour" to it, one further basic manoeuvre remains for the Neoclassical project: it *declares* that "rationality" generally characterizes the actual behaviour of real economic agents, that no less than the laws of the Supreme Being and historical materialism, this pattern of human behaviour is "context-independent" (Mayhew 1987, pp. 588-590).

The above described superstructure of the Neoclassical narrative, including the logical order of its development, is summarized as follows:

1. Equilibrium Hypothesis.
2. Individual Behaviour Hypothesis.
3. Justification of the Equilibrium and Individual Behaviour Hypotheses by:
    a. Deriving properties of individual behaviour consistent with the Equilibrium Hypothesis,
    b. The rhetorical manoeuvre of naming this set of properties "rationality",
    c. Assertion that "rationality" describes real economic agents.

In public, including in the training of economists, Neoclassical economics usually reads its models backwards. This gives the illusion that they show the behaviour of individual economic units determining sets of equilibrium values for markets and for whole economies. It hides the fact that these models have been constructed not by investigating the behaviour of individual agents, but rather by analysing the requirements of achieving a certain macro state, that is, a market or general equilibrium. *It is the behaviour found to be logically consistent with these hypothetical macro states that is prescribed for the individual agents, rather than the other way around.*[2] This macro-led analysis, this derivation of the micro from a macro assumption, is and always has been the standard analytical procedure of theory construction for the Neoclassical narrative. Sometimes, for pedagogical reasons, authors call attention to how the "individualist" rabbit really gets into the Neoclassical hat. For example, consider the following passage from a once widely used introduction to economics.

> "*For the purpose of our theory*, we want the preference ranking to have certain properties, which give it *a particular, useful structure. We build these properties up* by making a

[2] At the macroeconomic level, Neoclassical theorists these days usually drop the pretence that they are concerned with individual choice and adopt "the assumption that all individuals have the same utility function" (Arrow 1991, p. 201). This assumption of perfectly homogeneous agents is the theoretician's equivalent of the Stalinist dream. Alan Kirman, in his analysis of the cynical expediency of this approach, notes that "the assumption of a representative individual is far from innocent; it is the fiction by which macroeconomists can justify equilibrium analysis and provide pseudo-microfoundations" (Kirman 1992, p. 125).

> number of assumptions, first about the preference-indifference relation itself, and then about some aspects of the preference ranking to which it gives rise" (emphasis added) (Gravell and Rees 1981, p. 56).

In other words, it is not the behaviour of the individual agents that determines the model's overall structure, nor even the structure of the preference ranking. *Instead it is the macro requirement for a particular structure which dictates the behaviour attributed to the individual agents.*[3] The "purpose" of this "particular, useful structure" is to *rationalize* the macro "conclusion" assumed at the beginning of the exercise.[4] The resulting model shows micro phenomena determining macro phenomena, whereas, in fact, it is the starting point of the macro structure that has determined the behaviour of the model's micro elements. Likewise, "rationality" becomes something defined to meet the exigencies of a desired conclusion.[5]

---

[3] The economic psychologist Peter Lunt describes the situation as follows.

> "For work to be credible in economics, it has to work in principle, formally stated in terms that are usable in relation to the expected utility model. The validity of the data, indeed, the psychological plausibility of the account, is not quite but almost irrelevant. . . . [Economists] use selected propositions encoding specific effects as labels for putative psychological processes in rational decision making under uncertainty" (Lunt 1996, p. 280).

[4] This quasi-theological function of "rationality" for the Neoclassical narrative requires that the concept be protected from critique. Geoffrey Hodgson describes the defense as follows.

> "'Rationality' is one of its basic assumptions, placing itself in a position of dogmatic invulnerability: protected not merely by apparent horror for the alternatives, but by the denial of full status as an economist to all those that dare to question it. Indeed, in economic circles to question the idea that human agents are rational is to risk disapprobation, exile or worse. An economist who raises such questions is likely to be met by the accusation that he or she is abandoning 'economics' itself (Hodgson 1988, p. 74).

[5] My analysis of the Neoclassical project is broadly similar to Tony Lawson's in his *Economics and Reality* (1997) (see especially pages 100-2; see also Fullbrook 1998b), but with the difference that mine is more categorical about Neoclassicalism's macro starting point and its scholastic methodology. For example, where Lawson writes "[e]ssentially the object [of Neoclassicalism] has been to establish macro-level results on the basis of 'microfoundations'" (p. 308), I would write "essentially the object has been to *rationalize* macro-level *beliefs* on the basis of 'microfoundations'". Furthermore, the above allusion to scholastic methodology should be taken as literal rather than metaphoric. Scholasticism was characterized by the use of deductivism to develop a systematic presentation and defense of Christian belief. Likewise, today's Neoclassical mainstream is characterized by its use of deductivism to create a

Neoclassicalism's third axiom for "rationality": the Independence Axiom

Neoclassicalism equates rationality with three conditions which individual behaviour must, as a minimum, satisfy if the core belief in market equilibrium is to be rationalized. Two of these axioms, completeness and transitivity, are usually made explicit and require no explanation here. But Neoclassical discourse customarily leaves unstated its third axiom for "rationality". Indeed, this axiom remains so well-concealed that it even lacks an established name. The tacit axiom concerns the relation between the one and the many. In the words of John Hicks, "economics is not, in the end, much interested in the behaviour of single individuals. Its concern is with the behaviour of groups. A study of individual demand is only a means to the study of market demand" (Hicks, 1946[1939], p. 34). Under traditional Neoclassicalism, "[i]nstead of taking the market demand function as a primitive concept one derives market demand explicitly from individual demand behavior" (Hildenbrand 1989, p. 254). The derivation consists of a summation of the individual demand schedules (for the same product). *But these summations are logically possible only if the demand functions of the various individuals are independent of each other.* Oskar Morgenstern, half a century ago, diagnosed the problem as follows:

> "Collective demand is generally understood as a summation of individual demand schedules (for the same commodity)... It [this additivity] is only valid if the demand functions of the various individuals are independent of each other. This is clearly not true universally. Current theory possesses no methods that allow the construction of aggregate demand curves when the various constituent individual demand curves are not independent of each other. The problem

---

systematic presentation and defense of its belief in equilibrating economic systems. Scholasticism reconstructed Greek thought so as to make it consistent with and support Christian faith. Neoclassicalism has reconstructed the notion of "rationality" so as to make it consistent with and support Neoclassical faith in equilibria. Scholasticism subordinated philosophy to faith. Neoclassicalism subordinates economics to the consideration of economic phenomena consistent with its faith. Both Medieval philosophy and Neoclassical economics, after brilliant beginnings and productive middle years, declined into well-funded but sterile logic-chopping.

> does not even seem to have been put. If there is interdependence among individual demand functions, it is doubtful that aggregate or collective demand functions of the conventional type exist..." (Morgenstern 1948, p.175).

Consequently, traditional Neoclassical market demand functions implicitly assume absence of interdependence between the behaviors of individual agents. I will call this logical requirement of the Neoclassical model the *Independence Axiom.*

However, considerations of agents' interdependence do appear in "mainstream" literature, and some have broader relevance than just game-theoretic situations. For example, models exist which show an individual agent's preferences influenced by the behaviour of other agents. But without extending these exercises to market populations, which means providing aggregate summation functions, these endeavours remain at the level of statements about the behaviour of single individuals reacting to others rather than about the behaviour of groups. Therefore, these exercises stand off on their own, disconnected from Neoclassicalism's main theoretical framework and pursuit. Indeed the primary effect, if not the intention, of these exercises may be merely to further conceal the Independence Axiom (Ackerman 1997, p. 656; Strassman 1993, p. 64). In any case, most of these exercises derive from Game Theory which, as Kenneth Arrow reminds us, "is a very general notion of equilibrium" (Arrow 1983b, p. 113). Furthermore, although non-cooperative Game Theory may hold promise for the study of agent interdependence, to date most of its applications, instead of modelling interaction between populations of heterogeneous individuals, include only "representative" players. As Alan Kirman notes, "any such model begs the basic issue of analysing what will happen when different individuals with conflicting interests are involved" (Kirman, 1992, p. 132). Instead, its axioms, like those of the standard model imply "absence of mutual influences and, more generally, absence of all phenomena associated with crowd or fashion behaviour" (Dupuy 1998, p. 114).

5. Post-SMD rationality

More significant than Game Theory for the Neoclassical project and an illustration of narrative rationality in the making are the developments that have followed from the Sonnenschein impossibility theorem or, more generally, the SMD results (Sonnenschein, 1972, 1973; Mantel 1974, 1976; Debreu 1974). Rank-and-file Neoclassicalists may appear ignorant of the catastrophe that has befallen their enterprise, but its major players have made heroic efforts to salvage parts of the original model. These include jettisoning the concept of Neoclassical rationality.

Sonnenshein's theorem, refined by Mantel, Debreu and others, shows that the traditional postulates of individual rationality fail to deliver two key ingredients of the Neoclassical narrative: uniqueness and stability of competitive equilibrium (Grandmont 1992, p.2). "Even if the class of admissible preferences is restricted even further [than is customary], ... the appropriate properties cannot be obtained from assumptions on the individuals in the economy" (Kirman 1992, p. 122). The belief held for so long that they could, turns out to have been a "naive illusion" which (for the informed) the SMD results "destroyed, once and for all" (Hildenbrand 1994, p. ix).[6]

The aftermath of the SMD falsification (on purely logical grounds) illustrates this chapter's thesis that traditionally "economic rationality" is defined so as to justify some metaphysical or *a priori* belief at the heart of the narrative. In the post-SMD world, Neoclassical rationality no longer fulfils its doctrinal function of rationalizing belief in the narrative's ideal state of affairs. Instead its continued presence impedes development of new theoretical paraphernalia for restoration of belief in the central doctrine. For this reason Hildenbrand, Grandmont and other Neoclassical theorists have set about deconsecrating and defaming the narrative's traditional definition of "rationality". Their writings bristle with heresies that in pre-SMD times would

[6] The "chief implication" of the SMD discoveries, observes S. Abu Turab Rizvi, "is that the hypothesis of individual rationality, and the other assumptions made at the micro level, gives no guidance to an analysis of macro-level phenomena" (Rizvi 1994, p. 363). In other words, these results remove the *reason d'être* for Neoclassical rationality.

have cost them their places in the Neoclassical mainstream (Hildenbrand 1983, 1989, 1994; Grandmont 1987, 1992). Of these none is more powerful and more effective than their routine placement of the word "rationality" and it permutations in quotation marks. This punctuation pierces the pretence "that there is only one way of judging sanely", only one reasonable set of postulates. Nor are the reformists loath to call attention, as non-Neoclassicalists have long done, to the dire shortcomings of the axiomatic individualistic microeconomic approach. Hildenbrand concedes that "individual preference relations are not observable and we have no criterion to judge assumptions on preferences as 'reasonable'." (Hildenbrand, 1989, p. 257). And:

> "I am afraid that all properties that have been formulated so far for individual demand functions, for example, the hypothesis of utility maximization or the Weak Axiom of Revealed Preference ... , are entirely grounded on a priori reasonings" (Hildenbrand, 1994 p. 12).

Any genuine aspiration to rise above pseudo-science entails a willingness to minimize the use of *a priori* assumptions. And, adds Hildenbrand, when "they cannot be avoided, one should state them explicitly, rather than try to cover them with some pseudoscientific justification" (Hildenbrand 1994, p.14). Coming from a leading Neoclassicist, this is strong stuff. Grandmont carries the reform even further. He argues for an "alternative research strategy" that would

> "*reverse* the traditional Neoclassical research programme, and ... obtain some form of *aggregate rationality* ... by relying more on particular features of the distribution of behavioral characteristics among the members of the system under consideration. An important issue to investigate would then be how such macroeconomic distributions might arise *endogenously* from specific socioeconomic interactive processes involving for instance imitation and/or differentiation effects at the micro-level" (Grandmont 1992, p. 33).

These proposed changes, however, are more likely cosmetic than epistemological. The new Neoclassical research programme appears as committed to a specially defined rationality as the old one. It envisages not so much an empirical study of demand phenomena, one that lets the facts fall where they may, but rather a presentation procedure for selling a new set of ad hoc assumptions that yield a market demand function with the properties needed to save belief in the narrative's market equilibrium. Nevertheless, the intriguing possibility exists that, because of the SMD results, Neoclassicalism will at some point bifurcate. On the one hand, some Neoclassicalists will prefer to surrender their belief in "individual rationality" so that they can retain their belief in market equilibrium. But others will prefer to forego the latter so as to salvage the notion of "rational choice" and to continue to defend the doctrine of methodological individualism.

6. Game Theory rationality

"[O]ne of the central contributions of game theory," notes Joseph Stiglitz, "has been to make it clear that the 'rational' actor model is not only descriptively inaccurate (as earlier economists had charged), but internally incomplete and/or inconsistent" (Stiglitz 1991, p. 138). Or at least so it is when considered within the context of Game Theory and its equilibrium concepts. Neoclassical rationality, it turns out, fits poorly with game-theoretic techniques. Like with general equilibrium theory, Neoclassical rationality's partnership with Game Theory has soured with maturity. Game-theory economics' increasing independence and shift of focus toward the equilbriating process has exposed shortcomings in the rationality concept inherited from Neoclassicalism. This has spurred economists whose commitment to game-theoretic research exceeds their commitment to Neoclassical rationality to invent and assign a new meaning to the coveted symbol "rationality". Among these revisionists, Ken Binmore stands out. His much-cited "Modeling Rational Players" Part I and Part II (1987; 1988) develops a rationality concept designed to fit the Game Theory narrative, and so provides a fifth example of narrative rationality.

In his introduction, Binmore says that his reform program for rationality "is closely related to the distinction Simon (1976) draws between *substantive rationality* and *procedural rationality*" (1987, p. 180). At one level, this is an apt comparison. Like Simon's procedural rationality, Binmore proposes to substitute a rationality concept that admits imperfection and stages of approximation. But at another level, that which Simon calls "scientific style", the two reform programs could not be more different. Simon's concept of procedural rationality calls for economics "to concern itself ... with the *actual* processes of cognition, and with the limits on *the human organism* that give those processes their peculiar character" (emphasis added) (Simon p. 147). This requires "emphasis on detailed *empirical* exploration of complex algorithms of thought" (p. 147).

Binmore, by contrast to Simon but like Hildenbrand and Grandmont, builds his case for a new rationality concept on the ground that it is needed to preserve the internal integrity of a knowledge narrative, to rescue it from "intractable difficulties" (1987, p. 212). Empiricism enters neither into his diagnosis of the impasse nor his proposal for a cure. Firstly consider Binmore's identification of the problem.

After noting that the Neoclassicalists have "hijacked" the word "rational", Binmore argues for the assignment of a new meaning to the word "rational" *because* the Neoclassical concept ill-serves the narrative or research program that he favours. Binmore is never less than frank about his narrative motivation. The traditional axiomatic approach to rationality, he says, "leads to intractable difficulties for games with some dynamic structure." Likewise, naive Bayesian rationality "will not do for game theory" (Binmore 1987, pp. 212, 211). Traditional Game Theory reaches solutions by assuming that agents are axiomatically rational, and often too by assuming that it is common knowledge that all players are perfectly rational. But Game Theory also makes it its business to consider those "irrational sequences of acts" which form the dynamic process "by means of which rational behavior is achieved" (Binmore 1987, pp. 180-1). This requires an explicit "model of the thinking processes of the players," a model which traditional Game Theory lacks and which renders it "helpless in the face of the counterfactual" (1988, p. 10) Binmore's project is to work toward this model.

Simon's *procedural rationality* calls for turning away from "deductive reasoning within a tight system of axioms" to a "detailed *empirical exploration* of complex algorithms of thought" (Simon, p. 147, emphasis added). Binmore also wants to forego axiomatics. But in terms of "scientific style", Binmore's solution to the rationality problem clashes head-on with Simon's procedural rationality. In place of characterizing "rational" behavior axiomatically, Binmore treats it as "essentially *algorithmic*" or constructive and seeks "to model a rational player as a suitably programmed computing machine" (Binmore 1987, pp. 181, 204) This attempt "to model the thinking processes" conceives of agents as capable of mistakes and attributes the primary source of their mistakes "to imperfections *within the_reasoning process itself*" (1988, p. 10; 1987, p. 183). The Neoclassical notion of *instantaneously perfect* rationality is thereby abandoned. But the nature of Binmore's rationality concept differs fundamentally from Simon's. Binmore is not proposing "empirical exploration" to discover the "algorithms of thought", but rather is *a priori* declaring or assuming them to be those of a "suitably programmed computing machine", and where "suitably" means that it satisfies the needs of the game-theoretic narrative.

What is significant above all in the present context is that by substituting the model of a programmed computing machine for axiomatics, Binmore presumes, no less than does Neoclassical rationality, *a universal point of view* toward characterizing and judging the actions of others.

7. The dialectic of otherness and the politics of "rationality" and...

(a) ...double-bind situations[7]

One notable irony of the modern period is that Neoclassical economics, which prides itself on its methodological individualism, founded its notion of rationality on principles irredeemably holistic. In doing so it followed a long tradition whereby economists make acceptance of their theories the criterion

[7] This usage alludes not only to Gregory Bateson's concept of double bind, but also and more importantly to W. E. B. DuBois's prior concept of double consciousness, which drew on an already distinguished African American tradition of social thought (DuBois). Frederick Douglass' *Narrative of the Life of Frederick Douglass, an American Slave* (1845), contains cogent examples of what I call double-bind rationality. For an overview of Douglass' contribution, see Boxill 1997, pp. 125-30. For a brilliant analysis of the logical structures underlying double-bind rationality, see Piper 1997.

of economic rationality.[8] All five narratives examined above (the Physiocratic, the Marxist, the Neoclassical, the post-SMD Neoclassical and Game Theory) define or seek to define "rational behaviour" by economic agents as that which is consistent with their narrative's core beliefs.

These scholasticisms exemplify a more general malaise affecting narrative notions of "rational" when employed in a socio-economic context. The source of the difficulty, and which will be shown to lead to a *general* paradox, lies in *the inherent two-sided nature of rationality concepts*. As one observer notes, "[t]heories of rational action or decision theories function as both normative and descriptive theory," (Ferejohn 1998, p. 160) and this double role invariably extends to the word "rational" itself, whose mere sight or sound evokes meanings at both the normative and descriptive levels.[9] For everyone, not just Françoise Quesnay, the existence of the proverbial "madman" is inferred by the word "rational". It and its antonym, irrational, form part of the common and emotive currency of social politics. Basic categories of citizenship and personhood have always been framed, sometimes explicitly, with reference to notions of rationality. One notorious application led the authors of the Constitution of the United States of America to "conceiving of a slave imported from Africa as three-fifths of a person" (Piper 1997, 210-11). A standard justification for the subjugation of women has always been that it is claimed that, whether due to the will of God or the whim of Nature, they are not fully "rational" beings. As theoretically validated repositories of "irrationality", the *prima facia* case is strong that women should not vote or hold elected office, argue with men, lead men, voice their opinions in the public arena, teach in higher education, receive recognition for their achievements in economics, etc..

These inequities, however, represent only one side of *the politics of*

---

8 Infamously, psychoanalysis employs a similar tactic when it treats disbelief in Freudianism as evidence of neurosis.

9 The ambiguity surrounding the word "rational" in the economic context stems partly from the way practical reasoning (of which Neoclassical rationality is an example) differs from deductive reasoning and from economics failure to come to terms with these differences. John B. Davis has written an admirably lucid explication of these opaque difficulties (Davis, 1995). Whereas deductive reasoning concerns the relation of entailment, a relation of necessity, "practical reasoning prescribes, and is reasoning leading toward action" (Davis, p. 320).

rationality. There is also the problem of maintaining the social order which those politics define. Individuals assigned to categories of sub- or partial personhood must be discouraged from subversive behaviour, that is, from manifesting more than that degree of "rationality" commensurate with that assigned to their social group. Through the ages, guardians of societies have devised and deployed diverse methods of discouraging the development and display of "rationality" in selected populations. For example, the slave codes in the American South made it a crime for African Americans to read. Another example is provided by the fate of these same people after the Civil War, when they were expected to play the clown for whites. If they chose not to play this part, then they faced being whipped, cudgelled, burned-out, turned-out or even lynched.[10] Similarly, the traditional choices available to women have been framed within the politics of rationality. Patriarchies everywhere have established subtle, complex, and pervasive systems which reward girls and women for deferring to the "rationality" of their male contemporaries and punish them for not doing so. These dialectics of otherness, which function to identify some social groups as more or less rational than others, have been described and analyzed by innumerable women and minority writers.[11]

Given that human groups and individuals define themselves in imitation of and in contradistinction to others, double-bind rationality necessarily shades everyone's socio-economic reality. If a society is not perfectly homogeneous, then in so far as notions of rationality become common conventions or institutions in the broad sense, *they become part of decision making situations as well as of decision procedures*. This recursiveness of "rationality", leading to *double-bind situations of choice*, falls outside the logical range of ethnocentric Neoclassicism. Rationality may in each case

---

[10] "Few lynchings had anything to do with black-on-white rapes, real or imagined. This was usually the cover story invented by Southern whites intent on destroying black entrepreneurs or farmers they had deemed too successful and wished to eliminate from economic competition" (Harold Evans. *The American Century*, London: Jonathan Cape, 1998. Quoted in Harold Evans, "The Big Country", *The Times Magazine*, 7 November 1998, p. 24).

[11] "In a dialectic of racist imposition and creative response in the process of survival and reproduction, New World African descendants-become-Americans have had to form and perpetuate new ways for getting on with their lives. A recurrent feature of life in the racialized crucible has been the struggle to resolve major tensions infecting identity-formation and all that follows in their wake. ..." (Outlaw 1997, p. 68).

have a specific subjective character that depends on the individual's socio-economic situation and that commits him or her to interdependent, intransitive and/or incomplete choice behaviour. Without identifying the situational character of an individual's experience and understanding it from his or her point of view, we cannot know what, by any standard, is rational behaviour for them.

I will offer just one concrete example of double-bind choice situations for consumers. Although it is a true story, it could have come out of a novel by Toni Morrison or James Baldwin. A recurrent theme of Morrison's novels is how white-Americans attribute irrationality to African-Americans and the effects this has on the choices of the latter. Baldwin, writing from white society's point of view in an essay, described the predicament of his fellow African-Americans as follows:

> "...if he [the black man] breaks our sociological and sentimental image of him we are panic-stricken and we feel ourselves betrayed. When he violates his image, therefore, he stands in the greatest danger..." (Baldwin, 1997).

In the northern Midwest American town where I grew up, there was a zone of insufficient size in which African-Americans were required to live. Its houses were owned by white absentee landlords who in exchange for exorbitant rents maintained their properties in near perfect dilapidation. The white townspeople attributed the state of these houses not to the landlords but to their victims, who were judged to be (and we were taught this in school) mentally weak people who lived only for today, wasting their wages on frivolities and indulgences, because of their intellectual incapacity to budget and spend rationally.

At the end of the 1950s – I was an undergraduate in this university town at the time – a family of four escaped from the ghetto. Over a period of many years they had saved enough for a substantial down payment on a house, by some miracle obtained a mortgage, bought a house in a poor neighbourhood and then quietly moved in.

Immediately their lives descended into living Hell. Events culminated a few weeks later when their house – fortunately they were away – was literally burned to the ground. No one, so far as I know, was ever charged. Nor were the white middle classes shocked by the outcome. On the contrary. They were relieved, and not because they had feared that African-Americans might have moved into their pricey neighbourhoods, but rather because they were scandalized by the way this family's *consumer behaviour* had violated the accepted image of African-Americans and aware of the threat that it posed to the town's social order. By burning the one family out of house and home, everyone in the African-American community, the B-group, received a strong reminder of how irrational it would be for them it they partook in the "rational" consumer behaviour of the European-American community, the A-group.[12]

b. The paradox of universal rationality

I now want to bring into the foreground the real-world paradox around which these dialectics turn. However defined, "rational" and "irrational" economic behaviour refer to observable patterns of behaviour, that is, to empirical phenomena. But this comes at a cost for the theoretician. It means that such behaviour by an individual stands potentially open to scrutiny, not just by possibly neutral social scientists, but also and more significantly by the immediate society in which that person lives, works and consumes. Consider any concept of rationality defined as some pattern of observable behaviour **R** and such that behaviour which is not **R** is irrational behaviour **I**. Assume that a person **B** belongs to a social category (a B-group) whose members are punished by another social category (the A-group) for **R** and rewarded for **I**. Assume that **B** prefers the consequences of **I** to those of **R**, and therefore chooses to behave irrationally. Assume that the concept of

---

[12] Are double-bind situations open to modelling by game-theoretic methods? If so, it is not immediately clear how, given that a standard assumption of Game Theory is that all the players are univocally "rational" (Sugden 1991, p. 765). Indeed, as George J. Mailath notes, non-cooperative Game Theory and Neoclassical economics are built on the same "heroic assumptions" (Mailath 1998, p. 1347).[9] But a frontier for developing models of interacting agents, including double-bind situations, may lie in another direction, namely, "in nonlinear probability theory and in computer power", which together permit emphasis on initial conditions, including the historical social situation, as well as the modelling of systems in a state of constant change and without equilibrium points (Ormerod, Rosewell 1998, p. 507).

rationality includes the stipulation that a person chooses that behaviour whose consequences he or she prefers. Then under the concept of rationality it follows that it is irrational for **B** to behave rationally and vice versa.

This paradox arises because for the B-person the phenomenological facts surrounding choice are intermeshed with "rationality" as a socially operative normative concept.[13] But this concept dependence is not limited to B-group people. An A-group person's choice behaviour may also be influenced by a concept of rationality if they wish to be perceived by others as "rational".

The more formal paradoxes of Newcomb and Ellsberg, and also those of backwards induction (Dupuy, 1998), are posited in terms of a standard or universal subject. But the paradox considered here is substantive, in the sense that it arises when choice phenomena are considered in their socio-economic context. Even so, theoreticians can easily conceal this paradox by eliminating the B-person's viewpoint (the phenomenology of being a B-person) from the application of the rationality concept, or, what comes to virtually the same thing, by making membership of the A-group a "necessary condition for the intelligibility of behaviour". This sort of erasure from the perceptual field is, of course, what B-groups complain happens to them regularly.

The underlying logic at work here needs emphasis. The concept of *homo rationalis* (or rational "man") only becomes meaningful if *homo rationalis* and *homo sapiens* do **not** refer to co-extensive sets, or, more precisely, only if the extension of homo rationalis is a proper subset of the set of homo sapiens. Therefore, the postulation of the former, also postulates the non-empty set of *homo irrationalis*. It is this bifurcation of humanity that makes any narrative definition of "rationality" innately and unavoidably political.

[13] Socially operative normative concepts must not be confused with concepts which are normative in the sense that social scientists say that for their purposes they regard them as such, as for example when L. Savage says he sees the principle purpose of his rational-choice theory as normative (1954, p. 20).

8. The nature of the present critique

Beginning with Foley (1893) and Veblen (1909), so much of a critical nature has been written on the question of "rationality" in economics, that it seems advisable to call attention to how the present critique, beyond its focus on narrative frameworks, contrasts with earlier ones.

The nature of what follows, which has been influenced by Sofianou (1995) and Dow (1995), differs fundamentally from Amartya Sen's famous attack on Neoclassical rationality in "Rational Fools" ([1977]1982). Whereas Sen proceeds by calling into question the wisdom of the assumption that "every agent is actuated only by self-interest", the present critique operates wholly within the compass of economics' traditional "first principle" (p. 84). Consequently, my critique is less radical than Sen's in the sense that it proceeds within the customary parameters, but more radical in the sense that it shows the inadequacy of that conceptual framework for dealing with what it was designed to consider, that is, economic self-interest.[14]

The present critique's relation to Veblen's ([1909]1994) is more ambiguous. The "peculiar conventionalism of aims and standards" (p. 155) of modern markets identified by Veblen enters into some of the choice situations which this chapter identifies as problematic for traditional thinking. But whereas Veblen's emphasis is on the inadequacy of any hedonistic approach, mine is that *as a tool for hedonism, Neoclassical rationality is self-defeating across a wide and expanding spectrum of decision situations.*

[14] The appearance of Sen's famous paper has encouraged research into economic behaviour not exclusively motivated by self-interest. Three complementary strands of this trend stand out as particularly significant. Firstly, experimental research shows that any notion of "rationality" that includes only self-interested behaviour is not gender-neutral. (See especially, Seguino, Stevens and Luts 1996.) Secondly, the *economie des conventions* or "French intersubjectivists", especially as practised by Laurent Thévenot, seeks "to locate market relations within a broader range of justifiable forms of action" that includes forms of coordination not based on self-interest (Thévenot 1989, p. 147). This school, which includes Dupuy, Olivier Favereau, and Orléan has much to say about economic rationality. (For a critical view of their work on rationality, see Postel 1998.) Finally, the Swiss-centered "economics of reciprocity", led by Ernst Fehr, have produced many interesting papers combining experimental research with innovative theoretical structures (Fehr et. al. 1998; Falk and Fischbacher 1999).

Also, the deficiencies exposed below are in addition to Herbert Simon's recognition that in practice rationality is bounded by the computational and information-gathering capabilities of the agent (Simon, 1976). The present critique pertains to the axioms of Neoclassical rational choice when interpreted procedurally no less than when interpreted substantively.

A vast literature exists on logical paradoxes affecting Neoclassical rationality and/or its near relations (e.g., Newcomb's Paradox, Ellsberg's Paradox, Prisoner's Dilemma, Chain-Store Paradox, Deterrence Paradox, Backwards Induction Paradox, Toxin Puzzle). These critiques turn mainly on the internal logic of axiomatic rationality as revealed in interesting, but often contrived boundary situations. Undeniably, this approach is a boon to academic scholarship. It permits analytical arguments of unsurpassable elegance admitting no final resolution. (See especially Dupuy 1998.) But beyond its aesthetic and entertainment value, the effects of this approach seem largely hermetic. Although the critique that follows also is situational in approach, its seven testing situations are drawn from the commonality of everyday modern life. Furthermore, it is with the compatibility of the set of Neoclassical axioms with these real-life situations rather than with the internal coherency of an axiom set that is under investigation.

Paradoxically – and I want to emphasize this point – what follows need not be construed as an attack on Neoclassical rationality. This book with its pluralist persuasion implicitly recognizes that the Neoclassical explanation of behaviour has, proving one is willing to ignore the politics of rationality, its legitimate range of application, namely, all those egotistical choice situations that do not fall into the seven categories identified below (barring discovery of others). The problem lies not with Neoclassical rationality itself, but rather with its anti-pluralist interpretation – the insistence that it be treated as a universal explanation of economic choice so as to rationalize the belief in the narrative of a determinate, equilibrating and "optimal" economy. It is this mixture of the analytic with the quasi-theological, rather than either on its own, that does damage.

9. Non-narrative rationality

In one of the most discussed papers on the modern philosophy of mind, Thomas Nagel notes that "every subjective phenomenon is essentially connected with a single point of view" (Nagel [1974]1995, p. 161). This simple truth, Nagel shows, dooms to failure all attempts to grasp subjective experience by objective methods. Narrative rationality is one such attempt, especially Neoclassical rationality, which purports to describe from a universal point of view how one aspect of *subjective* experience, "satisfaction", can be maximized. Neoclassicalism's prescriptions, as noted, are precisely those which are logically consistent with its belief in the ubiquity of equilibria. Unsurprisingly, this procedure tags "rational" and "irrational" to personal economic behaviour in a manner which neither honours the diversity of human experience nor accords with the pleasures and expediencies of daily existence (Fullbrook 1997). So I am now going to identify seven categories of decision behaviour which Neoclassicalism regards as irrational – because they violate one or more of the axioms of independence, transitivity and completeness – but which are "common to the generality of men" and which from common-sense or non-dogmatic points of view merit the description "rational"[15] (Veblen 1994, p. 148).

a. Social being

The most pervasive of the classes of reasonable behaviour excluded from Neoclassical analysis are consumer choices made with regard to one's *social being*. To be a social being means to have regard, sometimes positive, sometimes negative, for the behaviour, opinion and companionship of others.[16] In a consumer society this regard inevitably extends to and

[15] Akin to non-narrative rationality is Lawson's "situational rationality"(Lawson 1997, pp. 187-8). This section's analysis can also be interpreted as a phenomenology-influenced example of what Paul Lewis and Jochen Runde call the "ontological turn", whereby those concerned with economics' foundations forego the traditional epistemological questions in favour of ontological ones, i.e., "investigating the assumptions that economists make about the nature of the entities and relations that make up the socio-economic realm" (Lewis and Runde 1999, p. 1).

[16] Even Neoclassicalism's more enlightened defenders are not above using animal metaphors to deride socially inspired choices. For example, in "Maximization and the Act of Choice" Amartya Sen writes: "In fact, 'herd behavior' not only has epistemic aspects of learning from others' choices (or being deluded by them . . .), but can also

mediates one's economic choices (Thévonot 1989). And who wishes to deny that it is patently absurd to think that to be a social being in a consumer society is irrational? Yet that is precisely what Neoclassical rationality infers when it insists that, given rational choice, the demands of individuals are independent of each other.[17] It also infers this through its transitivity condition, because regard for social being means that changes in the norms of one's reference groups lead to intransitive choices.

Consumption, like financial speculation, is not performed in isolation but instead is a social activity. For the most part the desires that fuel it are not determined by biological hunger, thirst and lust but instead are created and recreated through one's daily indeterminate experiences in an ever-changing social space. The mere fact that consumers are social beings – that "they care about each other" (Lavoie 1992, p. 75) – gives them many eminently sensible reasons for basing their choices, in part, on considerations of other peoples' choices. This is especially true in affluent, mass-communication and digitally-networked societies where consumer demand is based increasingly on a "desire to exchange in order to acquire a social identity, to be recognized by others" (Levy 1991, 11). Desire for social identity translates into consumer desires because commodities have non-material as well as material properties. Goods carry meanings, bundles of often

---

be linked with the possibility that joining a 'herd' makes the choice act less assertive and perspicuous" (Sen 1997, p. 751). Sen's long and meticulously meritorious paper also illustrates the Neoclassical practice of exhaustively treating anomalies that have been carefully chosen not for their significance but rather for their treatability in terms of the Neoclassical paradigm. Sen lavishes attention on two relatively minor lacunas in Neoclassical analysis of decisions ("chooser dependence" and "menu dependence") while ignoring all the major ones discussed in the present chapter. This is analogous to a doctor overlooking a patient's brain tumour, exploding appendix and broken leg in favour of treating their cold sores.

[17] Without this restriction individual demands are not additive and the Neoclassical model fails not only to deliver its equilibrium solution, but also to derive market demand functions. But whereas the transitivity, completeness, reflexivity, and continuity assumptions are usually made explicit, and likewise for strong monotonicity or local non-satiation and convexity assumptions where they apply, and also the Archimedean and substitution axioms when needed for choice under uncertainty, the *Independence Assumption*, the most reality-violating and theoretically strategic of them all, is often unstated. For example, Fedderke lists completeness, reflexivity, transitivity, continuity, strong monotonicity or local non-satiation, convexity and, for choice under uncertainty, substitution and Archimedean axioms, but makes no mention of independence (Fedderke 1997, pp. 340-1).

conflicting socio-cultural significances which change with the season and the social context and which arise from the market exchange process itself. These meanings affect consumers: "taste classifies and it classifies the classifier" (Bourdieu 1984, p. 8). Rational choice, therefore, requires choosers to give weight to these intersubjective, context specific, market-based kaleidoscopes of meanings. To be fashionably dressed, for example, means buying one's clothes with an eye to what other people are buying and to be ready and willing to take part in counter-trends (Foley 1893).[18] Likewise to dress so as to make oneself appear hireable, promotable, respectable, outrageous, youthful, and etc. requires giving weight to current and ever-changing consumer patterns. Everyday sociability also entails regard for the consumption decisions of others. To be conversable – surely not an irrational desire – often depends on buying and consuming the books, films, entertainments, newspapers and the like that the people one knows buy and consume. For most people, to enjoy a night out means patronizing businesses where other people are enjoying a night out. Rare is the person who does not find it expedient to look to the choices of other consumers as guides to what they might buy.[19] All these and other forms of imitation and interdependence enter into the decision processes of modern and post-modern consumers, from the youngest to the oldest, from the poorest to the richest, and from the rock star to the accountant, so that if these behaviours are not rational, then there exist no rational consumers, not even any who begin to or would want to approximate the Neoclassical ideal.

---

[18] And sometimes to be fashionably dressed means other things as well. "Do you still put your pants on over your shoes?" This was the headline of a series of advertisements run by J & F Suits in 1965 and 1966 in the American men's magazine GQ. The copy continued: "Don't admit it if you do. You shouldn't be able to. Any suit that calls itself new should have tapered pants so narrow you have to put your shoes on last" (Frank 1997, p. 197).

[19] Of course most of this and more was said rather better by Veblen a long time ago (1899). For example:

> "Ordinarily his [the consumer's] motive is a wish to conform to established usage, to avoid unfavourable notice and comment, to live up to the accepted cannons of decency in the kind, amount, and grade of goods consumed, as well as in the decorous employment of his time and effort. In the common run of cases this sense of prescriptive usage is present in the motives of the consumer and exerts a direct constraining force, especially as regards consumption carried on under the eyes of observers" (Veblen 1994, p. 71).

b. Reciprocal imitation

Keynes's theory of speculation identifies a market dominated by "a society of individuals each of whom is endeavouring to copy the others" (Keynes [1936]1973, p. 214). "*Reciprocal imitation*" (Dupuy 1989a) such as this has no place in Neoclassical rationality, but when confronted with a *self-referential market structure*, reasonableness requires the imitation of other agents who in turn are imitating other agents (Dupuy 1989c). Keynes attributed the emergence of reciprocal imitation in financial markets to institutional change. With the development of organised investment markets, "all sorts of considerations enter into the market valuation which are in no way relevant to the prospective yield" (Keynes [1936]1973, p. 152). In consequence, the market throws up a "conventional" but mercurial valuation based on the mass psychology of the agents operating in the market. This creates a situation where, if the investor cares about the future market value of his investment, rational decision must be based on the anticipated decisions of other investors. Jean-Pierre Dupuy notes that in these circumstances "[r]ationality and imitation are one and the same thing" (Dupuy, 1989b, p. 508). Here rationality requires behaviour contrary to the Neoclassical axiom of independence.

Although reciprocal imitation remains excluded from mainstream analysis, it continues to increase in relative importance. Fashion phenomena, whose cultivation of both intersubjective and intransitive choice was noted above with regard to social being, overlaps with the present category and grows in influence as societies gain in affluence. But still more ascendant, and more urgently in need of analytical attention, is the current rampant growth of reciprocal imitation in the world's financial markets. This surge, like the one in Keynes's day, comes as a direct consequence of institutional development. World-wide digital integration of stock and currency markets has globalized financial speculation. Electronic trading, hedge funds, and internationalized diversification of investment portfolios have created a global financial emporium in which reciprocal imitation dominates market decisions (Orléan 1997).

c. Self-referential goods

The well-known process of dematerialization leading to the development of fiat money has its parallel in the development of some contemporary consumer products. Consider the cola industry. Beginning in the 1960s, Pepsi-Cola abandoned attempts to create demand for its product on the basis of tangible properties (Frank 1997, pp. 169-172). It turned instead, with great success, to marketing Pepsi as a symbol of membership in its *own* population of users, that is, "the Pepsi People", "the Pepsi Generation". The company's advertisements and the demand which they generated can be understood only in terms of *symbol.* The efficacy of such symbols *as the basis of their own market demand* is founded on people believing that other people believe that the product represents certain values. Here the "communicative property of goods", whose meanings lead to the creation of market-value, arises directly through the market exchange process (Heap, 1989, p. 10). In such cases, the individualist point of view intersects with a holistic or collective one, giving rise to an "intersubjectively agreed social fact" (Runde 1998, p. 17). Rather than being mere curiosities, as Neoclassicalists claim, these and other interdependencies are central to modern consumer choice (Heap 1989, p. 98).

The chicaneries of soft-drink peddling might be dismissed as unwholesomely manipulative, but everyone concurs with the need to maintain confidence in modern dematerialized monetary systems. When money takes the form of inconvertible paper currency and bank deposits or merely digital codes, it exists as pure symbol, devoid of intrinsic value, a pure case of a *self-referential good.* Moreover, modern money has as its population of users the universal set of economic agents. Yet its very existence as a medium of exchange and store of value is irreconcilable with the basic axioms of the Neoclassical narrative. The confidence, André Orléan has shown, which is "an essential element in any analysis of money, is not reducible to a rational calculation in terms of utility" (Aglietta and Cartelier 1998, p. 131). Similarly, Geoffrey Ingham has demonstrated that "money is itself a social relation in the sense that it cannot be adequately conceptualized other than as the emergent property of a configuration (or 'structure') of social relations" (Ingham 1999, p. 177). Dematerialized money becomes fiduciary only through a process of intersubjectivity, and so lies beyond the explanatory power of Neoclassical rationality with its *keystone axiom of independence of individual demands*. Orléan, who emphasizes the non-contractual nature of money, accounts for modern money's exchangeability as follows:

> "What accounts for the acceptance of money is the *belief* that the future generation will accept in its turn this money and also all the generations to come. If individuals desire to hold on to money in the absence of any legal obligation which would protect them from non-reimbursement, it is in virtue of a chain of beliefs concerning the manner in which all individuals in the future will behave" (my translation) (Orléan 1998, p. 376).

This describes a market situation where every agent's demand for the commodity is wholly dependent on the demand for the same of other agents. Money comes to have value and individuals *choose* to accept it in exchange through this process of communal belief with its self-referential structure of universal imitation.

> "It takes the form of a belief concerning the behaviour of the community as a whole. In other words, the obligation of reimbursing the currency is supported by no one in particular, if it is not by the community as a whole" (my translation) (Orléan 1998, p. 376).

By kicking Neoclassical habits of thought, Orléan's approach to the monetary relation makes acceptance of dematerialized money intelligible as a rational choice.

d. Spontaneity

Neoclassical rationality is the progeny not only of a holistic vision, but also of the more austere times in which it emerged. If the margin between survival and death is precarious, the material means of life permitting only the narrowest existence, then unbending application of the hedonistic calculus may be the best strategy for making the most of one's prospects. But with the bettering of economic circumstance, come possibilities for enjoyment and enterprise ill-served or even irreconcilable with the application of the strictures of Neoclassical rationality. Keynes believed that this incongruence extended even to basic investment decisions. "If human nature", he notes, "felt no temptation to take a chance, no satisfaction (profit apart) in constructing a factory, a railway, a mine or a farm, there might not be much investment merely as a result of cold calculation" (Keynes [1936]1973, p. 150). But the conflict between the cold application of indifference maps and the pursuit of leisured pleasures is even more obvious and acute. The sybarite merely occupies the common perceptual ground in realizing that maintenance of preference consistency (transitivity) and estimation of outcomes up to the limits of one's cognitive powers (completeness) are not always consonant with "the good life". Indeed, allegiance to Neoclassical rationality precludes several major classes of consumer pleasures in today's "experience economy". These include choices motivated by spontaneity, by the spirit of adventure and by the wish for change.

Firstly, consider spontaneity. Keynes noted, and only a killjoy would beg to differ, some hedonistic activities depend on spontaneity (Keynes [1936]1973, p. 161). This means there exists a logical impasse for any notion of rationality that requires agents always to work to a plan. Jon Elster explains it nicely.

> "Take the plan to behave spontaneously. There is nothing incoherent in the end state which defines that plan, since people often do behave spontaneously. Yet trying to be spontaneous is a self-defeating plan, since the very act of trying will interfere with the goal. There is a possible world in which I behave spontaneously, but none in which I plan to do so and succeed (Elster 1985, p. 11).

Neoclassical rationality requires choices be made according to a preference ordering, a plan which, even when simplified to "procedural rationality", is extremely complex. Therefore, by the lights of the Neoclassical narrative, spontaneous consumption decisions and those people who make them are irrational. The joys of carnival, the pleasures of impulse buying, and the elation of lubricated but unpremeditated conviviality are examples of categories of consumer choice founded on spontaneity and, therefore, falling foul of the Neoclassical regime of good consumership. Existence of cultural differences between "races" regarding the value placed on spontaneity, means that the Neoclassical concept of rationality/irrationality is *not* a racially neutral construct. This is a simple but important fact with which Neoclassical economists of good will will be anxious to address.

e. Adventure

Neoclassical rationality assumes that decisions are or are ideally made with perfect knowledge of future outcomes or some approximation to it. *Adventure,* however, turns on ignorance. Without some absence of knowledge about what lies ahead, adventure is impossible. Its essence dwells in the unknownness of coming experience. Taste for this uncertainty is not confined to heroes and heroines. Shadows of Marco Polo and Amelia Earhart live in us all, making the pleasures of the unknown and the indeterminate universal. Even the elderly and the infirm enjoy reading a who-done-it or cliff-hanger. And even the tamest package holiday attracts with its promise of unknown experiences. The travel brochure's proverbial "400 cheeses to choose from", for example, aims at a consumer preference for the untried. Many everyday consumption decisions also take place under the influence of the desire for the unknown. Spectator sports, which form one of the world's largest industries, owe their massive appeal to the indeterminacy of their outcomes. Similarly, for someone to choose a product *because* they are ignorant of its properties is both commonplace and accepted as a reasonable criterion of consumer choice. No eyebrows are raised when someone says they are having zabaglione *because* they have never had it. Nor do you expect to be thought irrational if you order the "Ice Cream Surprise".

f. Free choice

As a logical system, Neoclassical rationality works by eliminating free choice from its conceptual space (Lawson, 1997, p. 8). It does so by proceeding on the basis of a temporal separation of the moments of preference ordering and of *what it calls* "choice". It defines rationality as people "choosing" what they *previously* decided or determined they prefer. Rationality requires, says Kenneth Arrow, that the agent's "choices be in conformity with an ordering or a scale of preferences" (Arrow [1952]1983a, p. 49). "[T]he individual is assumed to choose among the alternatives available that one which is highest on his ranking" (Arrow [1958]1984b, p. 56). "[R]ational behaviour simply means behaviour in accordance with some ordering of alternatives in terms of relative desirability..." (Arrow [1951]1984a, p. 7). This approach, notes the philosopher Donald Davidson, "has no predictive power at all unless it is assumed that beliefs and values do not change over time. The theory merely puts restrictions on a temporal cross-section of an agent's dispositions to choose"[20] (Davidson [1971]1995, p. 154). Only by separating the two acts – a prior ranking of goods (or ordering of priorities) and a subsequent buying of goods in the market place – do "irrationality" and "rationality" become distinguishable.[21] Without *the temporal gap*, irrational behaviour is impossible under the Neoclassical definition. Similarly, under the revealed preferences approach, "rationality" assumes that no change in preferences takes place for the period in which preferences are revealed.

So the basic condition of Neoclassical rationality is that individuals must forego choice in favour of some past reckoning, they must "act as utility-maximizing automata on the basis of given preferences" (Hodgson 1998, p. 28). This conceptual elimination of freedom of choice, in both its everyday and philosophical meanings, gives Neoclassical theory the hypothetical determinacy which its Newtonian inspired metaphysics require (Hodgson 1993, pp. 23, 217-8). *No indeterminacy; no choice. No determinacy; no Neoclassical narrative.*[22] Nor does Game Theory promise help here.[23] As

---

[20] Davidson's famous critique focuses on decision theory as invented by Frank Ramsey and "rediscovered" by Morgenstern and von Neumann (Davidson [1971]1995, p. 153).

[21] Likewise, "[f]or preferences to have explanatory power they must be sufficiently persistent to explain behaviors over time and across situations" (Bowles 1998, p. 79).

[22] Tony Lawson diagnoses the Neoclassical exclusion of free agents as follows.

> "In the formal 'models' found in mainstream journals and books, human choice is ultimately denied. For if real choice means anything it is that any individual could always have acted otherwise. And this is precisely what contemporary 'theorists' are unable to allow in their formalistic modelling. That is, although the reality of choice appears to be widely acknowledged by economists in their more informal discussions and public pronouncements, the exercise of choice is a phenomenon that is always absent from the formal substantive analyses that are conventionally reported. Instead, individuals are represented in such a way that, relative to their situations, there is almost always but one preferred or rational course of action and this is always followed. Despite some suggestive rhetoric,

Sheila Dow observes,

> "[g]ame theory derives propositions from its own formal models, on the basis of axioms which may differ from those of pure general equilibrium theory. But these axioms require that behaviour be depicted deterministically, just as in general equilibrium theory, in order for demonstrative solutions to be derived" (Dow 1995, p. 718).

The question of whether preference ordering is a complex act of choice or an event culturally determined in a strict sense falls outside the province of Neoclassical rationality, since it always takes preferences as given. But the question of what is the length of *the temporal gap* between the preference ordering and the market behaviour, although rarely mentioned, throws light on the theory's structure, especially on the murky whimsicality at its logical core. At one extreme, if the gap is negligible, say sixty seconds, then the claims that the theory is making for itself also are negligible. In this case anyone who sticks by a transitive preference ordering for a minute is 100 percent rational. But at the other extreme, the theoretician may think of the gap as being as long as a human life. He or she may think of rationality as, first, mapping out a set of preferences that takes in the whole of one's anticipated lifetime, and then sticking to it to the bitter end. But *a priori* it is neither more nor less rational to change one's mind about something after sixty seconds than it is after sixty years or after any intermediate period of time. Consequently, what is rational and irrational behaviour under the Neoclassical paradigm comes down, in the final analysis, to the individual economist's personal preference for the size of *the temporal gap*. As an argument, this leaves much to be desired.[24]

---

human doings, as modelled, could not have been otherwise" (Lawson, 1997, p. 8)

[23] "At the same time that non-cooperative game theory has become a standard tool in economics," notes Larry Samuelson, "the usefulness of game theory has been increasingly questioned" (Samuelson 1993, p. 313). He identifies the difficulties which Neoclassical rationality poses for game-theoretic models as one of two factors responsible for thwarting useful application of Game Theory to economics.

[24] For other but complementary ideas regarding free choice and preference change see Jonsson 1992, 1994 and 1996.

But however long one takes the temporal gap to be, postulation of a form of closed-mindedness, of being "set in one's ways", as the ultimate meaning of rational choice is a model that not everyone finds appealing. Except among the very old and the clinically neurotic, dogged consistency of choice has never, outside economic theory, cut much ice as a behavioral ideal. It is at odds with the contingency and indeterminacy of human existence, with the developmental character of a healthy personality, with the humanist tradition, and, most especially, with the temper of detraditionalized societies.

Choice takes place at particular points of time in the individual's life, so that what is "rational" is *relative* to those points. A person's phenomenal world changes continuously from birth to death. "Because today is today and tomorrow, tomorrow, I can no more look at my present from the point of view of the future than I can see the Earth from Sirius" (Merleau-Ponty [1945]1964, p. 46). If human life is a developmental process, then by definition one cannot know what one's points of view will be toward future choice situations. To imply otherwise, as the Neoclassical narrative does, is to indulge and encourage others in fantasy.

The temporal relativity of what is a "rational" choice for a person increases in post-traditional societies, where choice is understood as extending to the very self. This view has become widespread through the women's liberation movement, which centred itself on a conception of self that both admits the possibility and deems it rational for a person to choose a self different from the one which, thanks to society, they already possess ("One is not born, but rather becomes a woman"). This approach identifies self-identity as a narrative, usually structured by institutional patterns, but open to radical and intentional modification by the individual. Under this conception, self or self-identity is an ongoing reflexive project. By now, the concept of a reflexive, narrative-based self holds sway in large sections of contemporary society. Even mainstream and still male-dominated sociology has incorporated this construct (Beck [1986]1992; Giddens 1991).

But the rapid cultural uptake of the reflexive notion of self comes at a great cost to the Neoclassical doctrine of rationality. If self-identity is an ongoing, intentional, reflexive project of change – and, by implication, so too preference orderings and meta-preferences and meta-meta-preferences and so on – then there exists no ground for putting forward, on any timescale, consistency of choice as a maximizing principle. A further logical twist occurs when, as seems increasingly the case, people's consumption choices become "lifestyle" choices which are about choices of self-identity. When this becomes the case, market choices determine preferences, rather than the other way around.

g. Taste for change

But the convolutions of self-identity are not alone in turning consumer preference and choice into a reflexive process and, thereby, beyond the scope of Neoclassical rationality. Over a century ago Caroline Foley identified "the taste for change" as very widespread in motivating consumer choice, and, where material circumstances permit, a human universal (Foley 1893; Fullbrook 1998a). Foley's thesis that consumers frequently prefer something *because* hitherto they did not prefer it strikes, with the precision of a drone missile, the superstructure of the Neoclassical narrative. If a consumer has a taste for change, then some intransitivity of choice is a necessary condition for its gratification. As Foley emphasized, with the improvement of material circumstance, this taste comes increasingly into play as a criterion of consumer choice. In our time, vast industries – tourist, film, television, pop music and publishing – have prospered by catering directly to what Foley also called "*the law of variety in wants*" (p. 461). The consumer whom we all know, but whose existence Neoclassicalism does not recognize, will choose for their self any book off the rack in preference to the one which he or she preferred and chose last time.

h. Axiom violations

This section has considered seven broad categories of consumer decisions accepted as rational by contemporary society but which, analysis shows, violate one or more of the axioms of Neoclassical rationality.[25] These results together with those of double-bind situations are summarized in the following table.

---

[25] In conversation Jean-Pierre Dupuy has proposed the analysis of consumer interdependence at three levels: formation of preferences, acts of choice and satisfaction.

Axioms violated

Categories of decision behaviour	Transitivity	Completeness	Independence
Double-Bind Situations	X	X	X
Social Being	X		X
Reciprocal Imitation	X		X
Self-Referential Goods			X
Spontaneity	X	X	
Adventure		X	
Free Choice	X	X	
Taste for Change	X		

10. Conclusion

Projects to understand the logic of economic choice which do not engage with the phenomenology of the same are doomed to epistemological failure and axiomatic delusions for the same reasons as are also attempts to theorize about the natural world without observing it. Economics' interest in choice behaviour has in the main been so far removed from the spirit of empirical, let alone scientific, inquiry that perhaps the brief, tentative and provisional explorations of the previous section of this chapter into the phenomenology of economic choice will not be without some interest. Each of the aspects of consumer behaviour considered above is widespread today, more or less understood by marketing professions, and influential in market outcomes. What is intended by the term "non-narrative rationality" is nothing neither less nor more than that the identification of rational or reasonable economic behaviour should be regarded as an empirical task, rather than a logical one dictated by the *a priori* foundations of a knowledge narrative.

Projects to understand the logic of economic choice are also doomed if they do not avoid subordination to an antiquated and discredited theoretical framework. This is not easy. Neoclassicalism operates a successful programme of division and co-optation. By making the "mathematically well-behaved consumer" its standard, all others are regarded as deviant (Debreu,

1986, p. 1267). In consumer theory this leads to what Frank Ackerman calls the game of "what can you explain if you accept all of the standard assumptions except one?" and which is self-defeating, because "each round of the game begins anew" so that "results never accumulate into a comprehensive alternative framework" (p.656). Although writing in a different context, Diana Strassmann observations also are apropos.

> "As long as adherence to central stories determines theoretical importance, modifications that do not adhere to these stories will be marginalized and known in detail almost exclusively by those who specialize in them. Furthermore, specialists are unlikely to be aware of the full extent to which the prototype fails over a broad range of economic contexts. Because few economists learn much about research on the "fringes," modifications to core theories cannot be easily co-ordinated to allow for the development of a unified conception of problems with core economic metaphors" (Strassmann, 1993, p. 64).

In this chapter we have looked at the notions of economic rationality thrown up by five narratives: the Physiocratic, the Marxist, the Neoclassical, the post-SMD Neoclassical and Game Theory Each projects into the realm of the Ideal a reality that, in fact, is experienced by people situated in history, geography, society and, not least, the evolving stories of their individual lives. Against these contingencies of lived existence, these narratives substitute a transcendental Idea, an Idea conceived to accommodate the beliefs of the narrative's adherents, and which is indisputable because it is beyond the empirical. If this Idea is consistently contradicted by the behaviour of free and thoughtful flesh-and-blood agents, then it is the latter – we have been taught to believe – who are wrong and in need of reform.

Against this tradition of reification of theoretical presumptions, this chapter has identified, in addition to double-bind situations, seven categories of decision making behaviour which Neoclassical rationality counts as irrational, but which any person of good sense and good will would see as reasonable.[26] What is so eminently notable about these categories is that taken together they include, even without the modern monetary relation, a very large, growing and arguably already dominant share of the consumer and financial decisions made in advanced economies. Rather than being obscure or far-fetched exceptions to the general rule, they characterise mainstream economic practice. They await an economics which is not conceptually embarrassed by their existence.

---

[26] Thévonot has noted that in a complex universe there exists "a plurality of possible justifications of action" (Thévonot 1989, p. 148). Similarly, Davidson notes that every action's "reasonableness is only seen in the light of the reasons that explain it" (Davidson 1998, p. 7).

Chapter 6

What is the difference between theories about "economic man" and theories about rats?

With humanity now facing the possibility of ecological collapse, economics' Neoclassical narrative increasingly looks not only absurd but also recklessly dangerous. So it seems fitting to conclude this book with one more look at its *homo economicus*.

1. The Greek legacy

As with so many things, one must begin with the philosophers of Greek antiquity to find the beginnings of systematic thought on the nature of consumer desire. Already in Xenophon's *Oeconomics* there appears the concept of use-value as a *relation* between an object and a person, rather than as a property of the object (Chapter 1, Section 1). Using an imaginary dialogue between Socrates and Critobulus, Xenophon describes how in the hands of a flautist a flute has value, but not in the hands of someone who does not know how to play a flute.

> "That is to say, the same things are wealth and not wealth, according as one understands or does not understand how to use them. A flute, for example, is wealth to one who is competent to play it, but to an incompetent person it is no better than useless stones" (Socrates).
>
> "True—unless he sells it" (Critobulus) (11).
>
> "We now see that to persons who don't understand its use, a flute is wealth if they sell it, but not wealth if they keep it instead of selling" (Socrates).

Without the ability to use it, the most exquisite of musical instruments is only so much inert matter to its possessor. More generally Xenophon's parable of the flute shows that the use-value of "goods originate from their capacity to satisfy the need of he who possesses them" and that such use-values are "conditioned by the judgement of the subject" (Barbieri, 1992, p. 5). Because this concept of use-value as a relation between an object and a human subject is kindred to philosophy's view of knowledge as a relation between an object and a knowing subject, the history of the theory of use-value is entwined in theories of knowledge.

Among philosophers, disagreements regarding epistemology centre on the nature and extent of the roles of the two terms of the knowledge relation. Aristotle's empiricism and its famous British variant lie at one extreme, Platonic rationalism at the other, and, in between, all manner of more moderate positions. Because these epistemological debates have been taking place for 2500 years, it seems unlikely that the central issue will ever be resolved. But much more than just this philosophical issue is at stake. What is important in terms of social welfare is that philosophers, by having the courage to participate in free and open debates, provide a public forum for an ongoing conceptual critique of "knowledge". Because use-value, like knowledge, is understood as a relation between objects and a knowing subject, one might expect to find disputes roughly paralleling those of the theory of knowledge surrounding the idea of use-value. Like knowledge, the relational character of use-value invites argument over the nature and relative importance of the contributions of the object and of the human subject to its existence. Yet through the ages – and especially in our time – there has been a paucity of informed debate about the nature of the use-value *relation*.

This absence stems partly from the way the history of the ideas of use-value and exchange-value has been compromised by nationalism and by bias from English-speaking economists against non-English-language writers. For example, there is a tendency to credit Adam Smith with the distinction between use-value and exchange-value, when, in fact, he was merely conveying a long-established idea to his English readership. It is necessary to digress here momentarily to review the principal points regarding the emergence of theories of use-value.[1]

Xenophon's parable of the flute is not only subjectivist, it is also highly suggestive of the distinction between value in use and value in exchange. But it was Aristotle in his *Ethics*, his *Rhetoric* and his *Politics*, who first extensively explored value from the subjective point of view (Houmanidis, 1995, p. 19), and who contributed ideas on value which, filtered through the Enlightenment, became part of the foundational concepts of modern economics. The most well-known of these ideas comes from Aristotle's *Politics*:

> "Of everything which we possess there are two uses: both belong to the thing as such, but not in the same manner, for one is the proper, and the other the improper or secondary use of it. For example, a shoe is used for wear, and is used for exchange; both are uses of the shoe. He who gives a shoe in exchange for money or food to him who wants one, does indeed use the shoe as a shoe, but this is not its proper or primary purpose, for a shoe is not made to be an object of barter" (Book I, Part 9).

This example – well-known both to the French Encyclopedists and the figures of the Scottish Enlightenment – establishes clearly the distinction between use-value and exchange-value so central to modern economic thought.

Economics' debt to Aristotle for the distinction between the two categories of value, if not always fully acknowledged, is nevertheless well-known. The same cannot be said for the metaphysics which Aristotle offered in support of his concept of use-value. His theory of human pleasure is rarely, if ever, mentioned by economists, and yet via Locke, Bentham and Mill it entered very substantially into the metaphysics upon which Neoclassical demand theory is based. The *Nicomachean Ethics* offers not one but two accounts of the nature of pleasure, and it is the second of these, the one found in Book X, that is germane to the development of Neoclassical economics. Here

---

[1] This section is indebted to Houmanidis, 1978, 1992, 1994, 1995.

Aristotle identifies pleasure as the response to a stimulus, the result of an object acting ("stimulating") in a favourable way upon a sensory organ or the mind. Consider especially the following:

> "That pleasure is produced in respect to each sense is plain; for we speak of sights and sounds as pleasant. It is also plain that it arises most of all when both the sense is at its best and it is active in reference to an object which corresponds; when both object and perceiver are of the best there will always be pleasure, since the requisite agent and patient are both present" (Book X, Chapter iv).

This theory of pleasure is notable for the passive role it assigns the human being and for its notion that each sensory organ generates pleasure independently of the others.

2. Newton / Locke / Bentham

Aristotle's empiricism foreshadowed the radical empiricism of the seventeenth century and the metaphysics of Neoclassical economics. John Locke, the primary founder of radical empiricism, believed that ideas originate through external things acting on our senses, "knowledge inlets". When material objects stimulate our sense organs, they produce effects, called "sensations", in our consciousness. Locke called these sensations and our recollections of them "simple ideas". It follows, he argues in *An Essay Concerning Human Understanding*, that:

> "*simple* Ideas *are not fictions* of our Fancies, but the natural and regular productions of Things without us, really operating upon us; and so carry with them all the conformity which is intended..." (Book 4, Chapter 4, No. 4).

Locke claimed that all our ideas were either these simple ideas, for which we act as mere passive receptors, or composites of such ideas. Isaiah Berlin has described the profound influence of Newtonian physics on this model of the mind.

> "The mind was treated as if it were a box containing mental equivalents of the Newtonian particles... These 'ideas' are distinct and separate entities..., literally atomic, having their origin somewhere in the external world, dropping into the mind like so many grains of sand inside an hour glass; there they continue in isolation, or are compounded into complexes... (Berlin, 1956, p. 18).

Locke's identification of inertia as a fundamental property of the human individual, also seems inspired by an analogy with Newtonian mechanics. Newton's first law of motion, also called "the principle of inertia" (from Latin word meaning "idleness" or "laziness") is:

> "A body remains at rest or, if already in motion, remains in uniform motion with constant speed in a straight line, unless it is acted on by an unbalanced external force."

Locke claims *a priori* a similar principle of inertia for human beings, a view which continues to be profoundly influential in shaping economics. Consider the following passage from Locke's *Essay*.

> "3. The infinite wise Author of our being, ... to excite us to these actions of thinking and motion that we are capable of, has been pleased to join to several thoughts and several sensations a *perception of delight*. If this were wholly separated from all our outward sensations and inward thoughts, we should have no reason to prefer one thought or action to another, negligence to attention, or motion to rest. And so we should neither stir our bodies, nor employ our minds ... It has therefore pleased our wise Creator to annex to several objects and to the *ideas* which we receive from them, as also to several of our thoughts, a concomitant pleasure, and that in several objects, to several degrees: that those faculties which he had endowed us with might not remain wholly idle and unemployed by us.
> 4. *Pain* has the same efficacy and use to set us on work that pleasure has, ..." (Book 2, Chapter 7).

In other words, Locke – and through Locke, Neoclassical economics – assumes that, like material bodies, the human personality will not be brought into "motion" unless disturbed by extraneous forces, in this case, sensations bringing pleasure or pain. This metaphysics of the human personality attributes to every sensation a measure of pleasure or pain belonging to *a single scale* applicable equally to every experience and every moment of every person's life (2.21.31). It is this inbuilt system of reward and punishment which overcomes the inertia of the human personality. Locke insists repeatedly that without the impetus of sensory pleasure and pain no one would do anything.

The causal theory of perception, the principle of human inertia, and the doctrine that a pleasure-pain continuum is the cause and rationale of all human exertion, both mental and physical, combine to create a coherent metaphysics. But it is one whose realm of plausibility is severely restricted. Locke's metaphysical vision excludes the on-going *individuality* of human experience – that is, a person's perceptual field, including their goals, hopes, anticipations, knowledge, prejudices, social conditioning, etc.. All these existential and individual facts of life have no place in Locke's conception of perceptual experience as a simple relation between physical stimuli and physical organs. Furthermore, if we relinquish the idea that the individual human self is self-identical, that is unchanging like the Newtonian atom, then the pleasure/pain principle begins to look hopelessly inadequate as a comprehensive explanation of human behaviour. If we think of the individual instead as an *emergent phenomenon*, something continually in the making through intentional human effort and through interaction with other selves, as a kind of project which, short of death, is never completed, then the structure of human behaviour begins to look not nearly so simple as Locke would have us believe.

In *An Essay Concerning Human Understanding* Locke ignores these other aspects of human reality which, when seen, render its theory decidedly inadequate. In the context of his theory, its major omissions tend to go unnoticed because of the confusion which arises when one term or sign stands for two distinct but connected concepts. With reference to human beings, we commonly use the word "self" to signify two very different things. There is "self" in the *biological sense* of a life that extends from birth to death. A "self" in this sense is self-identical: a person remains the same person, for example Isaac Newton or Simone de Beauvoir, from one day to the next and for the whole of their life. But there also is "self" in the *existential sense* – of a being who is continuously in the making and who to some degree changes with each and every experience. An individual learns, grows up and grows old, acquires new sensibilities, finishes projects and begins new ones, amasses memories, changes their self-image, etc., etc.. When not engaged in life-and-death struggle, it is this *non-self-identical self* – not the biological self – which acts as the focal point of human life. Obviously, Locke's metaphysical system cannot accommodate this fundamental ambiguity of the human condition, so he includes only the biological self in his discussion of selfhood. He makes no mention of the existential self. By this omission Locke gains the confidence to declare: "consciousness . . . is *self* to *itself* now, and so will be the same *self* as far as the same consciousness can extend to actions past or to come" (3.27.10).

Locke's introverted, asocial, static, passive, inert, hedonistic, materialistic model of humankind became the basis of that set of presuppositions called *homo economicus*. The following passage from Locke's *Essay* encapsulates many of the main points of what was to become the key concept for the Neoclassicalists.

> "*Happiness*, then, in its full extent, is the utmost pleasure we are capable of, and *misery* the utmost pain; and the lowest degree of what can be called *happiness* is so much ease from all pain, and so much present pleasure, as without which anyone cannot be content. Now, because pleasure and pain are produced in us by the operation of certain objects either on our minds or our bodies and in different degrees, therefore, what has an aptness to produce pleasure in us we call *good*, and what is apt to produce pain in us we call *evil* . ... when they come in competition, the degrees also of pleasure and pain have justly a preference (2.21.42).

When, a century later, Jeremy Bentham sought to popularize these ideas under the banner of "utility", he began by merely paraphrasing Locke, substituting for the latter's "good", the word "utility". In *An Essay Concerning Human Understanding* Locke wrote as follows:

> "Things then are good or evil only in reference to pleasure or pain. That we call good which *is apt to cause or increase pleasure, or diminish pain in us, or else to procure or preserve us the possession of any other good or absence of any evil.* And, on the contrary, we name that *evil* which *is apt to produce or increase any pain, or diminish any pleasure in us, or else to procure us any evil, or deprive us of any good."* (2.20.2).

In his *An Introduction to the Principles of Morals and Legislation* (1789) Bentham reworded Locke's statement as follows:

> "By utility is meant that property in any object, whereby it tends to produce benefit, advantage, pleasure, good or happiness ... or ... to prevent the happening of mischief, pain, evil or unhappiness to the party whose interest is considered" (Chapter 1, Section 3).

3. Neoclassicalist fixation

The Lockean theory of human reality and, by implication, of use-value became the anvil of Neoclassical economics. This strategic function is especially obvious in Stanley Jevons's *The Theory of Political Economy* (1871), where, in his enormously influential Chapter III "The Theory of Utility", he establishes some of the fundamental preconceptions of the Neoclassical narrative by quoting Bentham's paraphrase of Locke (Jevons 1970, p. 102), and spelling out his own Lockean vision of the human being as a simple pleasure machine. Eric Roll notes that, via Bentham, Jevons "found ready at hand a complete philosophy whose aim was precisely the establishment of the principles of human action" (Roll 1973, p. 379). Jevons, believing in Bentham's theory of the human psyche, proceeded to list "*the laws* of human enjoyment" (italics added) (Jevons 1970, p. 102). Whereas ethical hedonism *advocates* the organization of one's whole life for the purpose of giving maximum pleasure, the Neoclassicalists, from Jevons onward, infer that such advocacy is utterly beside the point, since we all are programmed to behave like hedonists in any case. Belief in this psychological hedonism leaves the human being "without past or future ... abandoned in a static situation" (Houmanidis, 1994, p. 89). Furthermore, when embraced dogmatically by economists, this set of presuppositions works against the advancement of human knowledge, as it sweeps aside the larger part of economic phenomena from the field of systematic inquiry.

In the 21st century the concept of *homo economicus*, rather than being modernised or post-modernised or having its narrow metaphysical base extended, has tended to be pushed even further into its seventeenth-century shell as today's Neoclassicalism pursues dreams of even greater *a priori* purity. With the narrative's nearly totalitarian hold on the profession's institutions and its increasing disconnect from the real-world, the faithful's belief in its bizarre metaphysic of human reality shows no signs of weakening. Marooned in its introversion and intoxicated by its scientism and mesmerized by its narcissism, "the queen of the social sciences" has, with increasing cost to humanity, opted for a kitsch stage-show travesty of scientific practice.

Neoclassicalism's incessant cuddling of its "economic man" led it into a cul-de-sac a long time ago. The eminent philosopher of science, Alexander Rosenberg, observes that modern consumer theory does not enable us "to predict consumer behaviour any better than Adam Smith" (Rosenberg, 1994, p. 224). But in the discipline's inner sanctum, this state of affairs has long been plastered over with ostentatious scientism. John Hicks, at the beginning of his *A Revision of Demand Theory* (1956), sets out his metaphysical commitment with typical imperiousness and dressed in the best scientific vernacular.

> "The human individual only comes into plain economics as an entity which reacts in certain ways to certain stimuli; all that the Plain Economist needs to be interested in are *the laws* of his reactions" (italics added) (Hicks, 1956, p. 5).

Objects, goes the fable, cause sensations in human beings who throughout all of history make decisions exclusively on the basis of a set of preferences between the expected different sensations caused by different objects – preferences which are totally independent of the preferences of other human beings. A few years after Hicks' pronouncement, Kenneth Arrow's landmark paper "Utility and Expectation in Economic Behavior" (1963) took the sensationalist, sociocultural-isolationist view of economic reality to its definitive position. Arrow considers a pair of papers by Neal Miller on electric shock experiments with rats. Rats, says Arrow, have utility functions which they seek to maximize, and he concludes that the difference between theories about economic man and theories about rats "is probably more semantic than anything else" (Arrow, 1984, p. 135).

References

Ackerman, Frank (2002) "Flaws in the foundation: Consumer behavior and general equilibrium theory" in Edward Fullbrook (ed.) *Intersubjectivity in Economics: Agents and Structures*, London and New York: Routledge, pp. 56-70.

Ackerman, Frank (1997) "Consumed in Theory: Alternative Perspectives on the Economics of Consumption", *Journal of Economic Issues*, vol. XXXI, no. 3, September, pp. 651-664.

Adkins, Lisa (1998) "Feminist Theory and Economic Change", *Contemporary Feminist Theories,* eds. Stevi Jackson and Jackie Jones. Edinburgh: Edinburgh University Press.

Aglietta, Michel and André Orléan (2002) *La monnaie entre violence et confiance*, Paris: Odile Jacob.

Aglietta, Michel and Jean Cartelier (1998) "Order monétaire des économies de marché", *La Monnaie Souveraine*, eds. Michel Aglietta and André Orléan. Paris, Éditions Odile Jacob, pp. 129-58.

Akerlof, George (2002) "Behavioral Macroeconomics and Macroeconomic Behavior", *The American Economic Review*, June 2002, Vol. 92, No. 3, pp. 411-433.

Aristotle (1934) *Aristotle's Poetics & Rhetoric.* London: Dent and Sons.

Aristotle. *Nicomachean Ethics.*

Aristotle. *Politics.*

Aristotle. *Rhetoric.*

Armengaud, Françoise (2001) "Le matérialisme beauvoirien et la critique du naturalisme dans le Deuxième sexe: une "rupture épistémologiqe inachevée", *Cinquantenaire du Deuxième sexe*, eds, Christine Delphy and Sylvie Chaperon. Paris: Syllepse.

Arrow, Kenneth J. (1983a[1952]) "The Principle of Rationality in Collective Decisions", *Collected Papers of Kenneth J. Arrow: Volume 1: Social Choice and Justice.* Cambridge, Mass.: Harvard University Press, pp. 45-58.

Arrow, Kenneth J. (1983b [1968]) "General Equilibrium", *Collected Papers of Kenneth J. Arrow: Volume 2: General Equilibrium.* Cambridge, Mass.: Harvard University Press, pp. 107-32.

Arrow, Kenneth (1984[1963]) "Utility and Expectation in Economic Behavior", *Psychology: A Study of a Science,* vol. 6, (ed. S. Loch). New York: McGraw-Hill, Reprinted in *Collected Papers of Kenneth J. Arrow*, vol. 3. Cambridge Mass.: Harvard University Press, pp. 117-146.

Arrow, Kenneth J. (1984a[1951]) "Alternative Approaches to the Theory of Choice in Risk-Taking Situations", *Collected Papers of Kenneth J. Arrow: Volume 3: Individual Choice under Certainty and Uncertainty*. Cambridge, Mass.: Harvard University Press, pp. 5-41.

Arrow, Kenneth J. (1984b[1958]) "Utilities, Attitudes, Choices: A Review Note" *Collected Papers of Kenneth J. Arrow: Volume 3: Individual Choice under Certainty and Uncertainty*. Cambridge, Mass.: Harvard University Press, pp. 55-84.

Arrow, Kenneth, J. (1991) "Economic Theory and the Hypothesis of Rationality", *The New Palrave: The World of Economics*, pp. 198-210. London: Macmillan.

Barbieri, Gino (1992) "Economic Phenomenology in the Greek Philosophers", *Archives of Economic History,* Vol. II, No. 1, pp. 5-22.

Barker, Drucilla K and Susan Feiner (2003) Feminist Perspectives on Gender and the Economy, forthcoming, University of Michigan Press.

Beauvoir, de Simone, (2006) *Simone de Beauvoir: Diary of a Philosophy Student, Vol. 1*. Chicago, University of Illinois Press.

Beauvoir, Simone de (1968) *Force of Circumstance*. Harmondsworth, Middlesex: Penguin.

Beauvoir, Simone de (1989) *The Second Sex,* trans. H. M. Parshley. New York: Vantage.

Beauvoir, Simone de (1998[1948]) *American Day by Day* London: Victor Gollancz.

Beck, Ulrich (1992[1986]) *Risk Society: Towards a New Modernity*, trans. Mark Ritter. London: Sage.

Bell, Bernard W., Emily R. Grosholz and James B. Stewart, eds. (1996) *W.E.B. Du Bois on Race and Culture*. London: Routledge.

Bell, Bernard W. (1996) "Genealogical Shifts in Du Bois's Discourse on Double Consciousness as the Sign of African American Difference", *W.E.B. Du Bois on Race and Culture*, eds. Bernard W. Bell, Emily R. Grosholz and James B. Stewart. London: Routledge, pp. 87-110.

Bentham, Jeremy (1982[1789]) *An Introduction to the Principles of Morals and Legislation*. London: Methuen.

References

Bergson, Henri (1991[1896]) *Matter and Memory*, trans. N. M. Paul and W. S. Palmer, New York: Zone Books.

Berlin, Isaiah (1956) *The Age of Enlightenment.* New York: Mentor.

Berlin, Isaiah. (1978) *Karl Marx: His Life and Environment.* Oxford: Oxford Uni. Press.

Bhaskar, Roy (1986) *Scientific Realism and Human Emancipation.* London: Verso.

Bohm, David (1983) *Wholeness and the Implicate Order*, London: Routledge.

Borges, Jorge Luis (1975) "Of Exactitude in Science" in *A Universal History of Infamy.* London: Penguin, p. 131.

Bourdieu, Pierre (1984) *Distinction: A social Critique of the Judgement of Taste.* London: Routledge.

Bowles, Samuel (1998) "Endogenous Preferences: The Cultural Consequences of Markets and other Economic Institutions", *Journal of Economic Literature*, vol. XXXVI, March, pp. 75-111.

Boxill, Bernard (1997) "Two traditions in African American Political Philosophy", *African-American Perspectives and Philosophical traditions*, ed. John P. Pittman. London: Routledge.

Brentano, Franz (1995[1874]) *Psychology from an Empirical Standpoint*, trans. Rancurello and Terrell, London: Routledge.

Bulmer, R. (1973[1967]) "Why is the casowary not a bird? A problem of zoological taxonomy among the Karam of the New Guinea Highlands" in *Rules and Meaning*, edited by Mary Douglas. Harmondsworth, Middlesex: Penguin, pp. 167-93. Originally published in *Man*, new series, vol. 2, no. 1, March, pp. 2-25.

Chaperon, Sylvie (1997) "La deuxième Simone de Beauvoir", *Les Temps Modernes*, Avril-Mai, No. 593, pp. 110-141.

Davidson, Donald (1995[1971]) "Psychology as Philosophy", *Modern Philosophy of Mind*, ed. William Lyons. London: Everyman, pp. 148-58.

Davidson, Donald (1998) "Who Is Fooled", *Self-Deception and Paradoxes of Rationality*, ed. Jean-Pierre Dupuy. Stanford, California: CSLI Publications.

Davies, Paul (1995) *Superforce: The Search for a Grand Unified Theory of Nature.* London: Penguin.

Davis, John B. (1995) "Is Emotive Theory the Philosopher's Stone of the Ordinalist Revolution?" *Measurement, Quantification and Economic Analysis: Numeracy in Economics*, edited by Ingrid H. Rima, pp. 318-32. London: Routledge.

Davis, John B (2002) "Collective intentionality and individual behavior" in Edward Fullbrook (ed) *Intersubjectivity in Economics: Agents and Structures*, London and New York: Routledge, pp. 11-27.

Debreu, Gerard (1986) "Theoretic Models: Mathematical Form and Economic Content", *Econometrica*, vol. 54, no. 6 (November) pp. 1259-1270.

Debrew, Gerard (1974) "Excess Demand Functions", *Journal of Mathematical Economics*, vol. 1, pp. 15-23.

Delphy, Christine (1984) *Close to Home*. London: Hutchinson.

Delphy, Christine and Diana Leonard (1992) *Familiar Exploitation: A New Analysis of Marriage in Contemporary Western Society*. Oxford: Polity Press.

Descartes, René (1965[1637]) *A Discourse on Method*, trans. E. S. Haldane and G. R. T. Ross, New York: Washington Square Press.

Descartes, René (1970[1641]) "Mediations on First Philosophy" trans. E. Anscombe and P. T Geach in *Descartes Philosophical Writings*. London: The Open University.

Douglass, Frederick (1993[1845]) *Narrative of the Life of Frederick Douglass, An American Slave*. London: Everyman.

Dow, Sheila C. (1995) "The appeal of Neoclassical economics: some insights from Keynes's epistemology", *Cambridge Journal of Economics,* vol. 19, pp. 715-33.

Dow, Shelia C. (1990) "Beyond Dualism", *Cambridge Journal of Economics*, vol. 14, no. 2, pp. 143-158.

DuBois, W.E.B. (1992[1903])*The Souls of Black Folk*; reprinted in Howard Brotz (ed.), *African American Social and Political Thought 1850-1920*, 2nd. ed.. New Brunswick, N.J.: Transaction Publishers.

Dupré, John (1993) *The Disorder of Things*. Cambridge, Massachusetts: Harvard

Dupuy, Jean-Pierre (1989) "Convention et Common knowledge." *Revue économique*, no. 2 mars, pp. 361-400.

Dupuy, Jean-Pierre (1989b) "Self-Reference in Literature", *Poetics*, vol. 18, pp. 491-515.

Dupuy, Jean-Pierre (1989c) "Convention et Common knowledge", *Revue économique*, No. 2, mars, pp. 361-400.

Dupuy, Jean-Pierre (1991) *La panique*. Paris: Les empêcheurs de penser en round.

References

Dupuy, Jean-Pierre (1998) "Rationality and Self-Deception", *Self-Deception and Paradoxes of Rationality*, edited by Jean-Pierre Dupuy. Stanford, California: CSLI Publications, pp. 113-150.

Dupuy, Jean-Pierre (2002) "Market, Imitation and Tradition: Hayek vs. Keynes" in Edward Fullbrook (ed) *Intersubjectivity in Economics: Agents and Structures*. London and New York: Routledge, pp. 139-158.

Elias, Norbert (1978) *What Is Sociology?*, London: Hutchinson.

Elster, Jon (1985) *Sour Grapes: Studies in the Subversion of Rationality*. Cambridge: Cambridge University Press.

Falk, Armin and Urs Fischbacher (1999) "A Theory of Reciprocity", mimeo.

Fedderke, J. W. (1997) "The Source of Optimality in Action", *Cambridge Journal of Economics*, vol. 21, pp. 339-63.

Fehr Ernst, G. Kirchsteiger and A. Riedl (1998) "Gift Exchange and Reciprocity in Competitive Experimental Markets", *European Economic Review*, vol. 42, pp. 1-34.

Fehr, E. and K. Schmidt (1999) "A Theory of Fairness, Competition and Cooperation", *Quarterly Journal of Economics*, vol. 144, pp. 817-851.

Fehr, Ernst and Armin Falk (2002) "Reciprocal Fairness, Cooperation and Limits to Competition", in Edward Fullbrook (ed) *Intersubjectivity in Economics: Agents and Structures*, London and New York: Routledge, pp. 28-55.

Fehr, Ernst and Armin Falk (forthcoming) "Reciprocal Fairness, Cooperation and Limits to Competition", *Intersubjectivity in Economics*, edited by Edward Fullbrook. London: Routledge.

Feiner, Susan (ed.) (1994) *Race and Gender in the American Economy: Views Across the Spectrum*, New York: Prentice Hall.

Ferejohn, John (1998) "Cooperation and Time", *Self-Deception and Paradoxes of Rationality*, edited by Jean-Pierre Dupuy, pp. 151-62. Stanford, California: CSLI Publications.

Feyerabend, Paul (1970) "Against Method", *Minnesota Studies for the Philosophy of Science*, 4.

Fleetwood, Steve (1996) "Order without equilibrium: a critical realist interpretation of Hayek's notion of spontaneous order", *Cambridge Journal of Economics*, vol. 20, no. 6, November, pp. 729-48.

Foley, Carlone A. (1893) "Fashion," *Economic Journal*, vol. 3, September, pp. 458-474.

Foucault, Michel (1971) *The Order of Things*, trans. by Alan Sheridan-Smith. New York: Random House.

Frank, Thomas (1997) *The Conquest of Cool: Business Culture, counterculture, and Rise of Hip Consumerism*. Chicago: University of Chicago.

"The French Students' Petition" (2000), http://www.btinternet.com/~pae_news/texts/a-e-petition.htm and in *The Crisis in Economics*, edited by Edward Fullbrook. London: Routledge, 2003, pp. 13-14.

Fullbrook, Edward (1996) "Consumer Metaphysics: the Neoclassicists versus the Intersubjectivists", *Archives of Economic History*, vol. vii, no. 1, pp. 53-74.

Fullbrook, Edward (1997) "Post-Modernising Homo Economicus", *Just Postmodernism*, ed. Steven Earnshaw. Amsterdam and Atlanta: Rodopi, pp. 67-87.

Fullbrook, Edward (1998) "Caroline Foley and the Theory of Intersubjective Demand", *Journal of Economic Issues*, Vol. XXXII, No. 3, pp. 709-731.

Fullbrook, Edward (1998b) "Shifting the Mainstream: Lawson's Impetus", *Atlantic Economic Journal*, Vol. 26, No. 4, December, pp. 431-440.

Fullbrook, Edward (2001) "Conceptual Displacement: From the Natural to the Social", *Review of Political Economy*, Vol. LIX, No. 3, pp. 285-296.

Fullbrook, Edward (2002) "An intersubjective theory of value" in Edward Fullbrook (ed) *Intersubjectivity in Economics: Agents and Structures*. London and New York: Routledge, pp. 273-299.

Fullbrook, Kate and Edward Fullbrook (2000) "Beauvoirs Einfluss auf Sartre", *Man wird nicht als Frau geboren,* hrsg. Alice Schwarzer. Köln: Kiepenheure & Witsch, , pp. 257-271.

Fullbrook, Edward and Kate Fullbrook (2001) "*Le deuxieme sexe* á l'épreuve du genre lttéraire", *Cinquantenaire du Deuxième sexe*, eds, Christine Delphy and Sylvie Chaperon. Paris: Syllepse, pp. 97-104.

Gadrey, Jean (2004) 'What's wrong with GDP and growth? The need for alternative indicators', in: Edward Fullbrook (ed.), *A Guide to What's Wrong with Economics*, London: Anthem Press, pp. 265-6.

Gates, Henry Louis (1992) *Loose Canons: Notes on the Culture Wars*, New York: Oxford University Press.

Giddens Anthony (1991) *Modernity and Self-Identity: Self and Society in the Late Modern Age*. Cambridge: Polity.

Grandmont Jean-Michel (1987) "Notes and Comments: Distributions of Preferences and the 'Law of Demand'", *Econometrica,* Vol. 55, No. 1 January, pp. 155-61.

References

Grandmont Jean-Michel (1992) "Transformations of the Commodity Space, Behavioral Heterogeneity, and the Aggregation Problem", *Journal of Economic Theory*, Vol. 57, pp. 1-35.

Gravelle, Hugh and Rees, Ray (1981) *Microeconomics*. London and New York: Longman.

Hargreaves Heap, Shaun P. (2002) "'Everybody is talking about it': Intersubjectivity and the television industry" in Edward Fullbrook (ed.) *Intersubjectivity in Economics: Agents and Structures*, London and New York: Routledge, pp. 123-138.

Hawking, Stephen (1995) *A Brief History of Time: From the Big Bang to Black Holes*. London: Bantam Books.

Heap, Shaun Hargreaves (1989) *Rationality in Economics*. Oxford: Blackwell.

Hempel, Carl G. (1966) *Philosophy of Natural Science.* Englewood Cliffs, New Jersey: Prentice-Hall.

Hicks, J. R. (1946[1939]). *Value and Capital: An inquiry into some fundamental principles of economic theory*. 2nd ed.. Oxford: Clarendon Press.

Hicks, John (1956) *A Revision of Demand Theory*. Oxford: Oxford Uni. Press.

Hildenbrand, Werner (1989) "Facts and Ideas in Microeconomic Theory", *European Economic Review*, vol. 33, pp. 25-276.

Hildenbrand, Werner (1983) "On the 'Law of Demand'", *Econometrica*, Vol 51, No. 4 July, pp. 997-1019.

Hildenbrand, Werner (1994) *Market Demand: theory and empirical evidence*. Princeton University Press.

Hodgson, Geoffrey M. (1998) "Evolutionary and competence-based theories of the firm", *Journal of Economic Studies*, vol. 25, No. 1, pp. 25-56.

Hodgson, Geoffrey M. (1998) "The Approach of Institutional Economics", *Journal of Economic Literature*, Vol. XXXVI, March, pp. 166-192.

Hodgson, Geoffrey M. (2002) "Reconstitutive downward causation: Social structure and the development of individual agency" in Edward Fullbrook (ed) *Intersubjectivity in Economics: Agents and Structures*, London and New York: Routledge, pp. 159-180.

Hodgson, Geoffrey M. (1988) *Economics and Institutions*. Cambridge: Polity Press.

Hodgson, Geoffrey M. (1993) *Economics and Evolution*. Cambridge: Polity Press.

Hondrich, Ted (ed.) (1995) *The Oxford Companion to Philosophy*, Oxford: Oxford University Press.

Horton, Robin (1971[1967]) “African Traditional Thought and Western Science” in *Knowledge and Control*, edited by Michael F. D. Young. London: Open University, 208-66. Originally published in *Africa, Vol. XXXVII.*

Houmanidis, Lazaros (1978) “The Paradox of Value in Ferdinando Galiani”, *Wirtschaftskräfte und Wirtschaftswege,* IV, pp. 599-609.

Houmanidis, Lazaros (1992) “Xenophon’s Economic Ideas”, *Archives of Economic History,* vol. II, No. 1, pp. 79-102.

Houmanidis, Lazaros (1994) *Humanitarian Economics: A New Perspective of Social Economics.* Athens: Synchroni Ekdotiki.

Houmanidis, Lazaros (1995) “Aristotle On Value and Price”, *Archives of Economic History*, Vol. VI, No. 2, pp. 7-22.

Hume, David (1978[1739-40]) *A Treatise of Human Nature*, Oxford: Oxford University Press.

Hume, David, (1955[1748]) *An Inquiry Concerning Human Understanding*. New York: Library of Liberal Arts.

Ingham, Geoffrey (1999) “Money Is a Social Relation”, *Critical Realism in Economics*. London: Routledge, pp. 103-124.

James, Henry (1962) *The Art of the Novel*. New York: Scribner’s.

Jevons, Willaim Stanley (1970[1871]) *The Theory of Political Economy*, Harmondsworth, England: Pelican.

Jonsson, Petur O. (1992) “Choice, Consistency, and Utility Maximization: Reflections on the Concept of Rationality”, *The Journal of Economics*. vol. 18, pp. 119-126.

Jonsson, Petur O. (1996) “On Meta-Preferences and Incomplete Preference Maps”, *International Advances in Economic Research*, vol. 2, no. 2, May, pp. 112-19.

Jonsson, Petur O. (1994) “Social Influence and Individual Preferences: On Schumpeter’s Theory of Consumer Choice”, *Review of Social Economy*, vol. 52, no. 4, winter, pp. 301-314.

Kail, Michel (2001) “Pour un anti-naturalisme authentique, donc matérialiste”, *Cinquantenaire du Deuxième sexe*, eds, Christine Delphy and Sylvie Chaperon. Paris: Syllepse.

Kaul, Nitasha (2002) “A critical ‘post to critical realism”, *Cambridge Journal of Economics*, Vol. 26, No. 6, pp. 709-726.

Keynes, John Maynard (1936) *The General Theory of Employment, Interest and Money*, London: MacMillan.

References

Keynes, John Maynard (1937) "The General Theory of Employment, *The Quarterly Journal of Economics*, 51, pp. 209-223.

Kirman, Alan P. (1992) "Whom or What Does the Representative Individual Represent?" *Journal of Economic Perspectives*, vol. 6, no. 2, Spring, pp. 117-36.

Kuhn, Thomas. S. (1970[1962]) *The Structure of Scientific Revolutions*, 2nd edition. Chicago: University of Chicago Press.

Lafferty, Peter and Julian Rose (eds) (1994) *The Hutchinson Dictionary of Science*, Oxford: Helicon.

Lakatos, Imre (1970) "Falsification and the Methodology of Scientific Research Programmes" in *Criticism and the Growth of Knjowledge*, edited by Imre Kakatos and Alan Musgrave. Cambridge: CUP.

Lavoie, Marc (1992) *Foundations of Post-Keynesian Economic Analysis*. Elgar.

Lawson, Tony (1997) *Economics and Reality*, London: Routledge.

Lawson, Tony (1999) "What Has Realism Got to Do with It?", *Economics and Philosophy* vol. 15 pp. 269-282.

Levy, Thierry (1991) "Conventions et Fondements de l'Echange marchand et de la Monnaie". Mimeo.

Levy, Thierry (2002) "The Theory of Conventions and a New Theory of the Firm", in Edward Fullbrook (ed) *Intersubjectivity in Economics: Agents and Structures*, London and New York: Routledge, pp. 254-272.

Lewis, David (1969) *Convention*, Cambridge, Massachusetts: Harvard University Press.

Lewis, Paul (1999) "Metaphor and Critical Realism", *Critical Realism in Economics: Development and Debate*, ed. Steve Fleetwood. London: Routledge, pp. 83-102.

Lewis, Paul, Jochen Runde (1999) "A Critical Realist Perspective on Paul Davidson's Methodological Writings on – and Rhetorical Strategy for – Post Keynesian Economics", mimeo, Workshop on Realism and Economics, Kings College Cambridge.

Lewis, Paul and Jochen Runde (2002) Intersubjectivity in the socio-economic world: A Critical realist perspective" in Edward Fullbrook (ed) *Intersubjectivity in Economics: Agents and Structures*, London and New York: Routledge, pp. 198-215.

Locke, John (1993[1690]) A*n Essay Concerning Human Understanding*, London: Dent.

Lott, Tommy L. (1997) "Du Bois on the Invention of Race", *African-American Perspectives and Philosophical Traditions*, ed. John P. Pittman. London: Routledge, pp. 166-187.

Lunt, Peter (1996) "Rethinking the relationship between economics and psychology", *Journal of Economic Psychology*, vol. 17, pp. 275-287.

Mailath, George J. (1998) "Do People Play Nash Equilibrium? Lessons from Evolutionary Game Theory", *Journal of Economic Literature*, XXXVI, September, pp. 1347-1374.

Mantel, Rolf (1976) "Homothetic Preferences and Community Excess Demand Functions", *Journal of Economic Theory*, vol. 12, pp. 197-201.

Mantel, Rolf (1974) "On the Chracteriszation of Aggregate Excess Demand", *Journal of Economic Theory*, vol. 7, no. 3, pp. 348-53.

Marx, Karl (1976) *Preface and Introduction to a Contribution to the Critique of Political Economy*. Foreign Languages Press, Peking.

Marx, Karl (1975) *Wages, Price and Profit*. Foreign Language Press, Peking.

Mayhew, Anne (1987) "Culture: Core Concept Under Attack", *Journal of Economic Issues*, vol. XXI, no. 2, June, pp. 587-603.

Mayhew, Anne (2002) "All consumption is conspicuous" in Edward Fullbrook (ed) *Intersubjectivity in Economics: Agents and Structures*, London and New York: Routledge, pp. 43-55.

Merleau-Ponty, Maurice (1945) "Metaphysics and the Novel", *Sense and Non-Sense*, trans. Hubert L. Dreyfus and Patricia Allen Dreyfus. Evanston, IL.: Northwestern UP, 1964, pp. 26-40.

Mill, John Stuart (1893) *System of Logic*, 8th edition. London: Longmans.

Mirowski, Philip (1989) *More Heat Than Light*, New York: Cambridge University Press.

Morgenstern, Oskar. "Demand Theory Reconsidered", *The Quarterly Journal of Economics*, February 1948, pp. 165-201.

Myrdal, Gunnar, Richard Sterner, and Arnold Rose (1944) *An American Dilemma: The Negro Problem and Modern Democracy*. New York: Harper.

Nagel, Thomas (1995[1974]) "What is it Like to Be a Bat?" *Modern Philosophy of Mind*, edited by William Lyons. London: Everyman.

Nelson, Julie A. (1995) *Feminism, Objectivity and Economics*. London: Routledge.

References

Orléan, André (1989) "Pour une approche cognitive des conventions économiques." *Revue économique*, no. 2 mars, pp. 241-72.

Orléan, André (1990) "Le role des influences interpersonnelles dans la formation des cours boursieers." *Revue économique,* no. 5, septembre.

Orléan, André (1992) "Contagion des opinions et founctionnement des marchés financiers." *Revue économique* no. 4, julliet, pp. 685-98.

Orléan, André (1997) "Les cours sont le reflet des croyances partagées des acteurs finaciers", *Le Monde*, 5 November, p. 22.

Orléan, André (1998) "La monnaie autoréférentielle: réflexions sur les évolutions monétaires contemporaines" in Michel Aglietta and André Orléan (eds.) *La Monnaie Souveraine*, Paris: Odile Jacob, pp. 359-386.

Orléan, André (2003) "What Is a Collective Belief" in P. Bourgine and J.-P. Nadal (eds) *Cognitive Economics*, Berlin: Springer-Verlag, pp. 171-184.

Ormerod, Paul (2002) "Social networks and information" in Edward Fullbrook (ed.) *Intersubjectivity in Economics: Agents and Structures*, London and New York: Routledge, pp. 216-230.

Ormerod, Paul and Bridget Rosewell (1998) "Situational Analysis and the Concept of Equilibrium", *Philosophy of the Social Sciences*, vol. 28, no. 4, December, pp. 498-514.

Outlaw, Lucius (1997) "African, African American, Africana Philosophy", *African-American Perspectives and Philosophical Traditions*, ed. John P. Pittman. New York: Routledge, pp. 63-93.

Petit, Jean-Luc (1999) "Constitution by Movement: Husserl in Light of Recent Neurobiological Findings" in *Naturalizing Phenomenology: Issues in Contemporary Phenomenology and Cognitive Science*, Jean-Luc Petit et al. editors. Stanford, California: Stanford University Press, pp. 220-244.

Piaget, Jean (1973) *Main Trends in Interdisciplinary Research*. London: George Allen & Unwin.

Piper, Adrian M. S. (1997) "Xenophobia and Kantian Rationalism", *African-American Perspectives and Philosophical Traditions*, edited by John P. Pittman, pp. 188-232. New York: Routledge.

Popper Karl R. (1959[1934]) *The Logic of Scientific Discovery*. London: Hutchinson.

Popper Karl R. (1972) *Objective Knowledge*. Oxford: Clarendon Press.

Postel, Nicolas (1996) "L'économie des conventions: Une approche instrumentale de la rationalité individuelle," *Revue économique*, vol. 49, no. 6, novembre, pp. 1473-95.

Poster, Mark (1975) *Existential Marxism in Postwar France*, Princeton, New Jersey: Princeton University Press.

Putnam, Hilary (2004), *Ethics Without Ontology*, Cambridge, MA: Harvard University Press.

Quesnay, François (1949[1765]) "Natural Right" in *History of Economic Thought: Book of Readings*, translated by D. W. O'Connell, pp.97-102. New York: Barnes & Noble. Originally in *Journal de l'agriculture, du commerce et des finaces*, Sept.

Rawls, John (1971) *A Theory of Justice*. Cambridge, Mass: Harvard University Press.

Rizvi, S. Abu Turab (2002) "Adam Smith's sympathy: Towards a normative economics" in Edward Fullbrook (ed.) *Intersubjectivity in Economics: Agents and Structures*, London and New York: Routledge, pp. 241-253

Rizvi, S. Abu Turab (1994) "The microfoundations project in general equilibrium theory", *Cambridge Journal of Economics*, vol. 18, pp. 357-377.

Robbins, Lionel (1935) *An Essay on the Nature and Significance of Economic Science*. London: Macmillan,.

Robinson, Daniel N. (1986) *An Intellectual History of Psychology*. Madison, Wisconsin: University of Wisconsin Press.

Roll, Eric. (1973) *A History of Economic Thought*. London: Faber.

Rorty, Richard (1980) *Philosophy and Mirror of Nature*. Princeton, New Jersey: Princeton University Press.

R*osenberg*, Alexander (1994) "What Is The Cognitive Status of Economic Theory?", *New Directions in Economic Methodology*. London: Routledge, pp. 216-35.

Runde, Jochen (1998) "Information, Knowledge and Agency: The Information Theoretic Approach and the Austrians", mimeo, Workshop on Realism and Economics, Kings College Cambridge.

Runde, Jochen (1999) "On Popper, Probabilities and Propensities", *Critical Realism in Economics*, ed. Steve Fleetwood. London: Routledge, pp. 63-82.

Russell, Bertrand (1967[1912]) *The Problems of Philosophy*, Oxford: Oxford University Press.

Salam, Abdus, *Unification of Fundamental Forces*, Cambridge University Press, Cambridge, 1990, pp. 98-101.

Samuelson, Larry (2002) "Evolution and Game Theory", *Journal of Economic Perspectives*, Vol. 16, No. 2, Spring, pp. 47-66.

References

Samuelson, Larry (1993) "Recent Advances in Evolutionary Economics: Comments", *Economic Letters*, Vol. 42, pp. 313-19.

Savage, L. (1954) *The Foundations of Statistics*. New York.

Schelling, Thomas (1977[1960]) *The Strategy of Conflict"*, Oxford: Oxford University Press.

Seguino, Stephanie, Thomas Stevens and Mark A. Lutz (1996) "Gender and Cooperative Behavior: Economic Man Rides Alone", *Feminist Economics*, vol. 2, no. 1, pp. 1-21.

Sen, Amartya (1997) "Maximization and the Act of Choice", *Econometrica*, vol. 65, no. 4, July, pp. 745-79.

Sen, Amartya (1982[1977]) "Rational Fools: A Critique of the Behavioural Foundations of Economic Theory". *Choice , Welfare and Measurement*. Cambridge Mass.: Harvard University Press, pp. 84-106.

Shiller. R (1991) *Market Volatility*, Cambridge, Massachusetts: Massachusetts Institute of Technology Press.

Silberberg, Eugene (1990) *The Structure of Economics: A Mathematical Analysis*, 2nd ed. New York: McGraw Hill.

Simon, H. A. (1955) "A Behavioural Theory of Rational Choice", *Quarterly Journal of Economics*, vol. 69, pp. 99-118.

Simon, H. A. (1976) "From Substantive to Procedural Rationality", *Method and Appraisal in Economics*, edited by Spiro Latsis, pp. 129-148. Cambridge: Cambridge University Press.

Simons, Margaret A. (1999) *Beauvoir and "The Second Sex": Feminism, Race, and the Origins of Existentialism.* New York: Rowman & Littlefield.

Smith, Adam (1979[1776]) *The Wealth of Nations*, Harmondsworth, England: Pelican.

Söderbaum, Peter (2003) "Democracy and the Need for Pluralism in Economics", *The Crisis in Economics*, edited by Edward Fullbrook. London: Routledge, pp. 94-96.

Söderbaum, Peter (2004) "Economics as Ideology and the Need for Pluralism", *A Guide to What's Wrong With Economics*, edited by Edward Fullbrook. London: Anthem, pp. 158-168.

Sofianou, Evanthia (1995) "Post-modernism and the notion of rationality in economics", *Cambridge Journal of Economics*, vol. 19, no. 2, pp. 373-90.

Sonnenschein, Hugo (1973) "Do Walras' Indentity and Continuity Characterize the Class of Community Excess Demand Functions?", *Journal of Economic Theory*, vol. 6, pp. 345-54.

Sonnenschein, Hugo (1972) "Market Excess Demand Functions", *Econometrica,* vol. 40, no. 3, pp. 549-63.

Stiglitz, Joseph E. (2002a) "Information and the Change in the Paradigm in Economics", *The American Economic Review,* Vol. 92, No. 3, pp. 460-501.

Stiglitz, Joseph E. (2002b) "There Is No Invisible Hand", the *Guardian*, December 20, 2002.

Strassmann, Diana (1993) "Not a Free Market: The Rhetoric of Disciplinary Authority in Economics", *Beyond Economic Man: Feminist Theory and Economics*, eds. Marianne A. Ferber and Julie A. Nelson, pp. 54-68. Chicago: University of Chicago.

Sugden, Robert (1991) "Rational Cchoice: A Survey of Contributions from Economics and Philosophy", *The Economic Journal*, vol. 101, July, pp. 751-785.

Tambiah, S. J. (1969) "Animals are good to think and good to prohibit", *Ethnology*, vol. 8, no. 4, October, pp. 424-59.

Thévenot, Laurent (1989) "Équilibre et rationalité dans un univers complexe", Revue économique, vol. 40, March, pp. 147-197.

Thévenot, Laurent (2002) "Conventions of co-ordination and the framing of uncertainty" in Edward Fullbrook (ed.) *Intersubjectivity in Economics: Agents and Structures*, London and New York: Routledge, pp. 181-197.

Tidd, Ursula (1999) *Simone de Beauvoir: Gender and Testimony*. Cambridge: Cambridge University Press.

Veblen, Thorstein (1934[1894]) "The Economic Theory of Woman's Dress", *Popular Science Monthly, December, pp. 198-205.* Reprinted in *Essays in Our Changing Order*, ed. L. Ardzroomi, New York: Viking Press.

Veblen, Thorstein (1994[1909]) "The Limitations of Marginal Utility" *The Philosophy of Economics: An Anthology,* edited by Daniel M. Hausman, pp. 143-156. Cambridge: Cambridge University Press. Originally in *Journal of Political Economy* vol., 17, pp. 620-638

Veblen, Thorstein (1994[1899]) *The Theory of the Leisure Class*. New York: Dover.

Walras, Léon (1984[1874-77]) *Elements of Pure Economics: or the Theory of Social Wealth*, trans. William Jaffé, Philadelphia: Orion Editons.

Wittgenstein, Ludwig (1974[1921]) *Tractatus Logico-Philosophicus*. London: Routledge.

References

Worswick, Christopher (1972) "Is Progress in Economic Science Possible?", *Economic Journal*, vol. 82, issue 325, pp. 73-86.

Wynarczyk, Peter (2002) "The economics of criminal participation": Radical subjectivist and intersubjectivist critiques" in Edward Fullbrook (ed.) *Intersubjectivity in Economics: Agents and Structures*, London and New York: Routledge, pp. 105-121.

Xenophon, *Oeconomics.*

Name Index

Name index

CPSIA information can be obtained
at www.ICGtesting.com
Printed in the USA
LVOW13s1744191216
517952LV00003B/216/P

9 781848 902282